DESCRIPTION OF
The Retreat

AN INSTITUTION NEAR YORK FOR INSANE
PERSONS OF THE SOCIETY OF FRIENDS

CONTAINING AN ACCOUNT OF ITS ORIGIN AND
PROGRESS, THE MODES OF TREATMENT, AND
A STATEMENT OF CASES

By

SAMUEL TUKE

First Published in 1813
Now reprinted by photolithography
with an introduction by

RICHARD HUNTER
M.D., M.R.C.P., D.P.M.
AND
IDA MACALPINE
M.D., M.R.C.P.

Process Press

Published in this edition by
Process Press
26 Freegrove Road
London N7 9RQ

Introduction © 1964
Dr Richard Hunter and Dr Ida Macalpine

Foreword © 1996
Professor Kathleen Jones

ISBN 1 899209 04 2

Produced for Process Press by
Chase Production Services
Printed in Great Britain

PSYCHIATRIC MONOGRAPH SERIES: 7

DESCRIPTION OF THE RETREAT

SAMUEL TUKE

CONTENTS

ILLUSTRATIONS

SOURCES

OTHER THAN THOSE GIVEN IN THE TEXT

Allen, Oswald, *History of the York Dispensary*, York 1845

Archbishop of York and others, *Report of the Committee of Inquiry into the rules and management of the York Lunatic Asylum* [Doncaster 1814]

Burrows, George Mann, *An inquiry into certain errors relative to insanity; and their consequences; physical, moral and civil*, London 1820

Gray, Jonathan, *History of the York Lunatic Asylum*, York 1815

Higgins, Godfrey, *A letter to the Right Honourable Earl Fitzwilliam ... respecting the investigation ... into the abuses at the York Lunatic Asylum*, Doncaster 1814

———, *The Evidence taken before a Committee of the House of Commons respecting the Asylum at York; with observations and notes*, Doncaster 1816

A vindication of Mr. Higgins, from the charges of Corrector: including a sketch of recent transactions at the York Lunatic Asylum, York 1814

[Higgins, Godfrey] Memorandum. In: The Good Old Times, by Daniel Hack Tuke, *Journal of Mental Science*, 1870, **16**, 249–51

Hunt, Harold Capper, *A retired habitation. A history of the Retreat, York*, London 1932

Hunter, R. and Macalpine, Ida, *A Treatise on Madness by William Battie & Remarks on Dr. Battie's Treatise ... by John Monro ... A psychiatric controversy of the eighteenth century*, London 1962. Psychiatric Monograph Series: 3

——— *Three hundred years of psychiatry*, Oxford University Press, 1963

— Introduction to: *An inquiry concerning the indications of insanity ... by John Conolly*, London 1964, Psychiatric Monograph Series: 4

Reports and Minutes of Evidence from the Select Committee appointed to consider of Provision being made for the better Regulation of Madhouses, 1815–17

Semelaigne, René, *Aliénistes et philanthropes ... les Pinel et les Tuke*, Paris 1912

Thurnam, John, *Observations and essays on the statistics of insanity, and on establishments for the insane; to which are added the statistics of the Retreat, near York*, London 1845

— *The statistics of the Retreat ... exhibiting the experience of that institution ... from its establishment in 1796, to 1840*, York 1841 (introductory remarks by Samuel Tuke)

Tuke, Daniel Hack, *Family portraiture. Memoirs of Samuel Tuke, with notices of some of his ancestors and descendents*, London 1860, 2 vols.

— *Chapters in the history of the insane in the British Isles*, London 1882

— *The insane in the United States and Canada*, London 1885

— *Reform in the treatment of the insane. Early history of the Retreat, York; its objects and influence*, London 1892

[Samuel Tuke & others] *A sketch of the origin, progress, and present-state of the Retreat*, York 1828

Obituary of Samuel Tuke, *The Asylum Journal of Mental Science*, 1858, **4**, 165–88

Tylor, Charles, *Samuel Tuke; his life, work, and thoughts*, London 1900

Since this MS went to press Edwin Wolf 2nd, Librarian of the Library Company of Philadelphia, has been able to trace for us Samuel Tuke's article 'published in a periodical at Philadelphia' mentioned on page 3 and not previously identified. It is entitled 'Hints on the Treatment of Insane Persons' and appeared anonymously in *The Eclectic Repertory and Analytical Review*, number 5 of volume 2, October 1811, pp. 105–10.

FOREWORD
by Professor Kathleen Jones

SAMUEL TUKE's *Description of the Retreat* was first published in May 1813. In the early days of care in public asylums in Britain, it was required reading: the only book which explained in detail how to care for mentally ill people with kindness and humanity; but by the late 1830s, the new asylum doctors were beginning to write their own accounts of their work. Tuke's book never went to a second edition, and some forty years ago, I was told that there were only five copies known to English libraries. Fortunately one of them was in the Retreat, where I was able to read it under the demanding eye of a portrait of William Tuke, Samuel's grandfather. It made astonishing reading. Dr Richard Hunter and Dr Ida Macalpine did a service to the history of psychiatry when they published a facsimile edition in 1964 with their own introduction.

That introduction, which follows in the present edition, deals with the Tuke family history, how the book was written and the heroic story of the reform of the York Asylum, in which the Tukes played a major part. These events reached the national Press, and led to a Select Committee of the House of Commons which sat for two years and published three major reports. In 1815, Samuel Tuke led his grandfather, by then old and blind, into the House of Commons to give evidence, and the Select Committee gave a long and respectful hearing to them. The story is amply documented;[1] but four issues may be worth further consideration: how did the Retreat come to set up a system of management so much at variance with the medical practice

of the day? Why did Samuel Tuke write a book about it?
What did he mean by 'moral treatment'? And why did a
book which had so much to offer in the way of enlightened
treatment go out of print?

Samuel Tuke describes how the Retreat was set up. The
immediate cause was the death of 'a female of the Society of
Friends' in 'an establishment for insane persons in the vicinity of the City of York'.[2] Her family lived at some distance
from York, and had recommended her to the care of the
Friends; but when they tried to visit her, they were told that
she was 'not in a suitable state to be seen by strangers', and
she died in circumstances which aroused strong suspicions of
ill-treatment and neglect. Samuel Tuke does not mention her
name, which was Hannah Mills, or the place where she died,
which was the York Asylum. Treatment of mentally ill people
at that time was generally harsh and brutal. They were assumed to be without reason, and therefore less than human.
Even the unfortunate King George III was subjected to a
régime of pain and humiliation – shackled with mechanical
restraints, intimidated and 'reduced' by bleeding, blisters and
purges. The Friends, with their commitment to non-violence,
were deeply concerned about Hannah Mills, but they had no
intention of raising a public outcry. They made their protest
quietly, by example and witness.

The new establishment was agreed at the Quarterly Meeting of the Society of Friends in March 1792, after some mis-
givings on the part of members. It was intended initially for
'persons of our own Society' though it was soon extended to
others recommended by Quakers. Treatment would be according to the tenets of the Society: that is, patients would be
cared for with gentleness and respect, and without bullying or
violence. The name of the Retreat was suggested by William's
daughter-in-law, Mrs Henry Tuke, as 'a quiet haven in which
the shattered bark might find the means of reparation or of
safety'.[3]

At this time, Quakers were a society apart. William Penn,

who published an account of the movement in 1811,[4] referred
to them as 'this despised people called Quakers'. They did not
'marry out'. They held aloof from the power of the state and
the established Church, refusing to stand for parliament, to
become magistrates, or to pay tithes. Few of them entered the
professions. In 1811, they still could not gain degrees from the
only two universities in England: Oxford required students to
subscribe to the Thirty-Nine Articles, and Cambridge refused
to let dissenters graduate. A few went to Edinburgh or Heidelberg, but for most, commerce was the only possibility of a
career. They were good, honest merchants, and often very
successful. They retained their plain, peaceful, sober, literal
ways, distrusted the clergy and the medical profession alike,
and went their own way.

The 'family establishment' of the Retreat had an apothecary as superintendent, and a separate lady superintendent.
They married in 1806, and this enhanced the family atmosphere. William Tuke acted as 'the father of the family', and
medical attention came from a visiting physician, Dr
Fowler, who had little experience of treating the insane.
This turned out to be a distinct advantage, because he had
an open mind; and after trying out the bleeding, blisters
and purges which were the only medical methods of the
day, he came to the same conclusion as William Tuke:
these methods simply did not work. Kindness, good food, a
glass of wine or porter, occupation and friendship produced
better results. The approach was purely pragmatic. They
were not challenging the medical profession, and they had
no talent for philosophising about what they were doing;
but they lived in the Age of Reason. They believed that
their patients were not wholly inaccessible to rational
thought. They were also deeply religious. They held that all
men and women were children of God and possessed the
'inner light' – the instinctive knowledge of the difference
between good and evil.

It seems likely that William Tuke always intended that

there should be some kind of publication. The records of the Retreat, from the time of the first decision at the Quarterly Meeting in 1792, were preserved methodically, with great attention to detail. All the documents are still in existence – the minutes of meetings, the plans, the accounts, the patient registers with records of patients admitted by age, sex, date of admission, date of discharge and prognosis, the case-books with long descriptions of patients' behaviour and the responses of staff, the 'Visiters' Book' with records of distinguished visitors and their reactions to the establishment. When Samuel Tuke first set quill pen to paper in January 1811, nearly twenty years of detailed records were available to him. He had no need of fresh research on the Retreat: his main task was précis. William Tuke may initially have intended to write the book himself, but by that time he was over eighty and losing his sight. The task devolved on his grandson, the member of the family whose interest in the subject most nearly matched his own.

By 1811, it was important to get something into print. Parliament had passed the County Asylums Act three years earlier, enabling local justices of the peace to erect public asylums for 'lunatics' from the prisons and workhouses. Though this was only a permissive Act, several counties were already drawing up plans for asylums – the Nottingham, Bedford and Norfolk Asylums were all open before 1815. Medical superintendents were appointed to these asylums because no other profession was available to take the responsibility, and many of the patients needed medical attention. They were admitted in a very debilitated condition – often half-starved, dirty, flea-bitten and suffering from a variety of untreated physical illnesses. It was time for the Retreat system of management to be set down in a form which would be helpful to these new asylum doctors, and which would convince the medical profession of its value.

Samuel Tuke approached this task diligently, and with

intelligence. He quoted all the leading medical specialists in insanity of his day – Ferriar of Manchester, Battie of St Luke's, Monro, Haslam and Crowther of Bethlem. The work of these last three must have made for grim reading, with their emphasis on confinement and brutality as the means of 'gaining ascendancy over the patients'. Samuel recorded what the Retreat had done, and with what results, in dry, detailed prose suitable for men of science; and he entirely omitted the *raison d'être* of the whole exercise: the fact that the Retreat was run on Christianity and common sense. This would not have commended it to the medical establishment, and he evidently wanted to avoid sectarian debate.

The new system needed a name: he found 'moral treatment' in a translation of a text by an eminent French physician, Dr Philippe Pinel. Evidently Samuel Tuke did not read French, and unfortunately the translation was somewhat inaccurate. The confusion between Dr Pinel's work in Paris and the Tukes' work in York still persists.[5]

Pinel's treatise[6] used the term *traitement moral*, and the translator, Dr David Daniel Davis, translated this as 'moral treatment'. He had no particular knowledge of the subject, and eventually became a gynaecologist.[7] But 'moral treatment is not the exact equivalent of *traitement moral* which means 'treatment through the emotions'. Pinel's work was in many ways quite alien to the system at the Retreat.

Pinel was the medical superintendent of the two great gloomy Paris asylums, Bicêtre and the Salpétrière. The fact that he struck the chains off some of the patients in these establishments in 1792, the year in which the Retreat was first planned, is sheer coincidence. Britain and France were at war, and France was at the height of the Revolution. Pinel acted on the orders of the revolutionary Assemblée Nationale. Striking off the chains was a symbolic enactment of Rousseau's 'Man is born free, and is everywhere in chains'.

Pinel's 'treatment through the emotions' was a humanitarian version of 'medical ascendancy'. Patients must trust their doctor, have confidence in their doctor, do what their doctor told them. He too was heroic in his way. He developed a one-to-one relationship with some of the toughest patients in what were probably the worst asylums in France; but his work was very different from what was being done in an English provincial city by a small religious sect. The Retreat was a homely place, small and supportive: in the full meaning of the words, a *Society*, and a Society of *Friends*.

According to Daniel Hack Tuke, Samuel's younger son and the first of William Tuke's descendants to qualify as a medical practitioner (after much family opposition), Pinel first heard of the Retreat through Dr Delarive, a Swiss medical practitioner who visited it in 1798.[8] Either this report did not reach Pinel in time to modify his comments in the *Treatise*, published three years later, or he did not think this largely non-medical experiment worth mentioning. Hack Tuke makes the point that 'the course of English and French reform in the treatment of the insane was entirely distinct and independent'.[9]

It is tempting to wonder if the confusion between the two systems could have been avoided if *traitement* in French had been a feminine noun instead of a masculine one. Confronted with *traitement morale*, Dr Davis might have understood that the appeal was to the emotions and not to the moral sense.

But for good or ill, Samuel Tuke picked up Davis's phrase, and called the Retreat system 'moral treatment'. His book was published in May 1813. Six months later, Godfrey Higgins, a gentleman of Skellow Grange, near Wakefield began his investigation into the York Asylum. Through the intransigence of Dr Best, the support of the editor of the *York Herald*, the fire, the death of four patients and the enlistment of Higgins, the Tukes and their allies as Governors, a very bad institution was put to rights, and a national reform movement started.

Dr Hunter and Dr Macalpine describe the enthusiastic initial reception of the Description of the Retreat, the Rev. Sydney Smith's commendation in the Edinburgh Review, the influence of the Retreat's system on the writing and practice of the early asylum doctors in Britain and America. Then the story goes quiet. The first edition of the book sold out within three years, and there was talk of a second, but it was never published.

The key to this seems to lie in Dr George Man Burrows' comment that he 'viewed with regret the little confidence professed by the benevolent conductors . . . in . . . the great efficacy of medicine in the majority of cases of insanity'.[10] The asylum doctors had become a specialist group within the medical profession, and the connection with a largely non-medical system run by a Christian sect had become an uneasy one. If 'moral management' was the same as *traitement moral*, why should they not quote Pinel instead? France was no longer an enemy, and Pinel's medical credentials were impeccable.

So Dr Robert Gardiner Hill, who abolished mechanical restraint in the Lincoln Asylum in the 1830s, wrote that he 'wished to complete that which Pinel had begun'.[11] Dr W.A.F. Browne, whose ambitious work on the past, present and future of asylums was published in 1837, wrote 'Unfortunately, every country does not possess a Pinel'.[12] Dr Burrows, whose massive textbook appeared in the following year, acknowledged a whole series of forerunners from Hippocrates to Pinel – but the only mention of the Retreat is a brief one in the section headed 'Religious Communication'.[13] The first edition of the *Asylum Journal*, the predecessor to the *British Journal of Psychiatry*, published in 1853, began with a tribute to Pinel in its opening sentence. There was no mention of the Retreat at all.

Those were the early days, when psychiatrists were on the defensive. Today they are well-established in medicine and work in partnership with other professional groups.

They and many other workers in the field of mental health may find it valuable to look at 'moral treatment' in its original English setting. The respect for patients, the emphasis on human rights and the value placed on relationships are as relevant now as they were in 1813.

NOTES

1. House of Commons, *Report of the Select Committee on Madhouses, 1815–16*: first report, 1815, Parliamentary Papers series, Irish University Press edition: Health – Mental vol. 1 pp. 1–10 and 129–44. Godfrey Higgins, *A Letter to the Right Honourable Earl FitzWilliam respecting the Investigation which has lately taken place into the Abuses of the York Lunatic Asylum, together with Various Letters, reports etc.* Rivington, London 1814. This volume contains Minutes of the Governors' meetings of the York Asylum, newspaper correspondence and other relevant material.
2. Samuel Tuke gives the date of Hannah Mills' death as 1791. H.C. Hunt, *A Retired Habitation: a history of the Retreat at York*, H.K. Lewis, London, 1832; p. 5 quotes the order for her grave to be dug in the Friends Burying Ground in York. This gives the date of her death as 30 April 1790.
3. Daniel Hack Tuke, *Chapters in the History of the Insane in the British Isles*, Kegan Paul, Trench, London, 1882 p. 115; H.C. Hunt, op. cit., p. 16.
4. William Penn, *A Brief Account of the Rise and Progress of the People called Quakers*, Phillips, London, 1811. See also a modern assessment by Fiona Godlee, 'Aspects of Non-conformity: Quakers and the lunatic fringe' in W. F. Bynum, Roy Porter and Michael Shepherd, *The Anatomy of Madness: essays in the History of Psychiatry*, Tavistock, London vol. II, 1987 pp. 73-85
5. See, for example, Michel Foucault's *Folie et déraison: histoire de la folie à l'âge classique*, Plon, Paris, 1961, trans. R. Howard as *Madness and Civilization*, Tavistock, London, 1979, pp. 241-78; Andrew Scull, *Madhouses, Mad-doctors and Madmen*, University of Pennsylvania Press, Philadelphia, 1981 p. 302; W. F. Bynum, 'Rationales for Therapy in British Psychiatry, 1780-1835' in

Scull, op. cit. p. 42; Roy Porter, *A Social History of Madness*, Weidenfeld and Nicolson, London, 1987.

6. Philippe Pinel, *Traité medico-philosophique sur l'aliénation mentale*, Paris, 1801, trans. David Daniel Davis as *A Treatise on Insanity*, Cadell and Davies, London, 1806.

7. See Paul Cranfield's preface to his edition of Davis's translation, Hafner, New York, 1962.

8. Hack Tuke, op.cit. p. 117. For the views of Dr Delarive, see the appendix to Samuel Tuke's *Description*, pp. 221–7.

9. Hack Tuke, op.cit. p. 118.

10. See R. Hunter and I. Macalpine, Introduction p. 23.

11. R. Gardiner Hill, preface to *A Lecture on the Management of Lunatic Asylums and the Treatment of the Insane*, Simpkin Marshall, London, 1839.

12. W.A.F. Browne, *What Asylums Were, Are and Ought to Be*, Adam and Charles Black, Edinburgh, 1837 p. 139.

13. George Man Burrows, *The Causes, Forms, Symptoms and Treatment of Insanity, Medical and Moral*, Underwood, London, 1838, p. 679.

INTRODUCTION

LIFE

SAMUEL TUKE was born on 31 July 1784, the second child of Henry Tuke and Mary Maria Scott and their only son to live to maturity. The Tukes were 'of the burgher or citizen class' and the name first appears in York in the 17th century when an ancestor suffered imprisonment for embracing the Quaker faith. Samuel's grandfather William (1732–1822) who founded the family firm of wholesale tea and coffee merchants, founded also the Retreat to which he, his son Henry (1755–1814) and his grandson Samuel devoted their lives, in addition to their many other religious and philanthropic labours.

Of his father Samuel wrote he 'was a man of sound, clear understanding, possessing a considerable share of energy ... his temperament was warm or sanguine, with a slight touch of the melancholic'; of his mother that

> Never were parent and child bound more fondly together ... She was much interested in the Establishment of the Retreat, and she gave it its name ... to convey their idea of what such an establishment should be, viz: a place in which the unhappy might obtain a refuge – a quiet haven in which the shattered bark might find the means of reparation or of safety.[1]

Of himself Samuel wrote 'I was a delicate child with a good deal of nervous debility, acutely sensible to pain of body, and the subject of lively religious impressions'. His mother called him 'the sweet harmonious Samuel'. He started schooling in the Friends' Girl School at York founded by grandfather and grandmother Tuke; at the age of eight he was sent to Ackworth, the Quaker School which William Tuke also helped to establish, and in 1795 to George Blaxland's at Hitchin. When he returned home in 1798 he wanted, like his father before him, to go to Edinburgh to study medicine. 'There can be no doubt that many of his mental characteristics peculiarly fitted him for the medical profession' wrote his son Daniel.[2] Instead he was pressed into the family firm where

---

[1] This name was adopted by the Society in 1793 as: The Retreat for Persons afflicted with Disorders of the Mind, or simply 'The Retreat'.

[2] Daniel Hack Tuke (1827–95), M.D. Heidelberg, F.R.C.P., editor of his father's memoirs and the first of the family to enter the medical profession. Before he took up medical studies at St. Bartholomew's Hospital in London in 1850, he acted for two years as secretary and house steward of the Retreat (1847–9). This office was founded after the passing of the *Act for the Regulation of the Care and Treatment of Lunatics*, 1845 which required the resident superintendent to be a medical man (the first at the Retreat was Dr. John Thurnam). In 1854 he became visiting physician to the Retreat, and later also to the York Dispensary and lecturer on mental diseases at the York School of Medicine. In 1858 with Sir John Bucknill he brought out *A manual of psychological medicine* which at once became the standard textbook and reached a fourth edition in 1879. Ill health forced him to retire in 1861, when the close association of the Tukes with their Retreat came to an end. Resuming work in 1875 he set up in London as consulting physician in mental diseases and lecturer at Charing Cross Hospital. He was one of the founders of the After-Care Association, joint editor of the *Journal of Mental Science* and president of the (Royal) Medico-Psychological Association, 1881. In 1882 he published his classic *Chapters in the history of the insane in the British Isles*, and in 1892 *A dictionary of psychological medicine* assembling a galaxy of international contributors, which remains the best guide to all aspects of later 19th century psychiatry.

'he appears to have soon acquired business habits, and to have steadily applied himself to the duties which devolved upon him'.

In 1807 he first demonstrated his sturdy independence and conviction of purpose when on behalf of William Tuke & Company he subscribed £50 towards William Wilberforce's election expenses without consulting his elders who were away in London. 'Samuel's bold stroke' wrote Henry Tuke 'gave his grandfather and me some surprise ... Friends are generally disposed to discourage this kind of interference [in political affairs]'. But soon because of the great anti-slavery issue, they all actively campaigned for him and years later Wilberforce spoke of 'My old friend Mr. Tuke – he is a second William Penn; indeed there are three in succession'.

On 14 June 1810 he married Priscilla, eldest daughter of James Hack of Chichester by whom he had twelve children. He devoted his life to his faith, his family, his business, and to the improvement of the conditions of the poor, the sick and the oppressed. His philanthropic interests ranged from the York Dispensary and Hospital to the Faithful Female Servants' Society, from anti-slavery to Irish relief and Catholic emancipation, from popular education to prison reform, from provident societies to temperance movements. But living in the atmosphere of the Retreat, itself a family concern, he devoted himself above all to the care and conditions of the insane.

The first relevant entry in his diary occurs in October 1810:

> Intend to collect all the knowledge I can on the theory of insanity, the treatment of the insane and the construction of lunatic asylums. For this purpose to collect and compare *facts* rather than *books*. Also to avail myself of any opportunity of ascertaining the state of lunatic paupers in places where I may happen to travel and report the accounts, along with those I already possess, to the editor of the 'Philanthropist'.

He was already familiar with the works of John Locke, David Hartley, Thomas Reid, Dugald Stewart, and with Blackstone's *Commentaries on the laws of England*, all of which have their place in the history of psychiatry.[1]

DESCRIPTION OF THE RETREAT

Preparation

On 3 January 1811 he entered significantly: 'Began, at my father's request, an attempt towards a history and general account of the Retreat. Such an account is much wanted. I shall not be able to do justice to it (if I can at all) without giving most of my leisure time to it, and therefore intend to drop attention to Hebrew at present, and read authors on the subject of insanity'. Four days later he made 'selections from Pinel' using Davis's translation of 1806; and 'had George Jepson [superintendent of the Retreat, see Note to page x] to dinner, and had much conversation on the subject of insanity'. He sketched the sections 'on moral treatment

---

[1] For details see Hunter & Macalpine *Three hundred years of psychiatry*, 1963.

of the Retreat' and 'on medical treatment and diet'; started 'Dr. Crichton on Insanity'[1]; noted 'that in Leeds and Scarboro' the insane poor have no distinct provision'; picked up 'Dr. Haslam's "Essay on Insanity" '[2] and looked 'Crichton's work over a second time'.

In March he wrote an 'Essay on the state of the Insane poor' which appeared in the *The Philanthropist; or Repository for Hints and Suggestions calculated to promote the Comfort and Happiness of Man*[3] (1811, **1**, 357-60):

> The professed objects of the conductors of the Philanthropist lead me to believe that the state of the insane poor in this country is a subject which will not be deemed inconsistent with the general tendency of their benevolent undertaking ... unhappily the attention of the public has never been properly directed to the miseries which our indigent fellow-creatures, labouring under the ... calamity of mental disorder have so long, and do continue to suffer.

He described 'an accidental visit to a workhouse in a city in the South of England'—perhaps Chichester, the home of his in-laws—where he saw in an outhouse lunatics lying in straw in mid-winter, their only access to light and air being through iron gratings in the doors. He concluded his little essay by regretting that counties had not been directed to provide asylums: 'might not the act [Wynn's Act, 1808] have obliged, instead of permitting magistrates to provide suitable accommodation for the insane poor?'—a measure enforced only in the Act of 1845.

At this time also in response to an enquiry, he sent off 'some remarks for the American Friends, who propose establishing a house for the insane, on the treatment of those labouring under this complaint, drawn from the experience of the Retreat'. His account 'attracted considerable attention ... and was published in a periodical at Philadelphia'. On treatment he advised that 'general bleeding and other evacuants have been found injurious ... and are therefore not used except when their necessity is indicated by the state of the bodily habit; cupping, however, is not infrequently resorted to'. Indeed, the gradual abandonment of these age old methods was accelerated by the evidence of the Retreat that patients got better more quickly without. Samuel Tuke was greatly encouraged to get on with his book by enquiries such as this.

In October he had done sufficient preparatory work to write 'for History of Retreat, in which I now propose to proceed'. By then a growing number of visitors were coming to study its methods like 'Morris and his wife who have undertaken the superintendence of an institution for the insane at Nottingham and are now studying the proper mode of treatment at the Retreat. A young man from Ireland (John Allen) who is likely to superintend the Irish Retreat, is also here upon a similar errand. This affords a prospect of our doing some good beyond our own sphere'—

---

[1] Sir Alexander Crichton's *An inquiry into the nature and origin of mental derangement*, 2 volumes, 1798.

[2] John Haslam's *Observations on madness and melancholy*, 1809, the second edition of *Observations on insanity* 1798.

[3] This journal which ran from 1811 to 1817 was founded and edited by that remarkable Quaker, philanthropist and scientist William Allen (1770-1843), F.R.S. and lecturer in chemistry at Guy's Hospital.

a statement which reveals how little the Tukes realised that they were initiating a new era. 'The early conductors ... pursued their admirable course with a simplicity, almost amounting to unconsciousness of what they were accomplishing' wrote Samuel Tuke of these heroic years in his *Review of the early history of the Retreat* appended to its 50th Report, 1846.

The first American doctor to visit the Retreat was John W. Francis of New York who wrote in the Visitors' Book on 30 November 1815:

> J. W. Francis is not wholly ignorant of the State of the Lunatic Asylums in North America, and he has visited almost all the institutions for the insane ... in England. He now embraces this opportunity of stating ... that this establishment far surpasses anything of the kind he has elsewhere seen, and that it reflects equal credit on the wisdom and humanity of its conductors. Perhaps it is no inconsiderable honour to add that institutions of a similar nature and on the same plan are organizing in different parts of the United States. The New World cannot do better than imitate the old so far as concerns the management of those who labour under mental derangement.

On 28 December Samuel had 'Finished No. 1 of History of Retreat' – presumably the first chapter. He continued his reading with Bryan Crowther's *Practical remarks on insanity; to which is added, a commentary on the dissection of the brains of maniacs*, 1811 and James Parkinson's *Mad-houses. Observations on the Act for regulating mad-houses*, 1811, both of which had just appeared. Next he read the section 'of insanity' in John Ferriar's *Medical histories and reflections*, 1795, volume 2, and 'Dr. Beddoes'[1] from which he 'made extracts on diet, warm bathing &c.' Among his other texts were the accounts of asylum architecture by William Stark and Robert Reid, both early visitors to the Retreat; *Report from the Select Committee appointed to enquire into the state of lunatics*, 1807; and William Battie's *Treatise on madness* and John Monro's *Remarks on Dr. Battie's Treatise*, both 1758.

Early in 1812 he was 'too much occupied in business to make progress', but by April was back at his task: 'Read Dr. Arnold on Insanity'.[2] In May he put together 'the chief part of chapter on moral treatment of insanity at Retreat', and incidentally recorded the assassination of Spencer Perceval by a madman, an event which his father, on a visit to the House of Commons, missed by half an hour.

During this year he paid a visit to St. Luke's Hospital for Lunaticks in London in order to discuss the 'humane system' with Thomas Dunston, the Master or Superintendent. Tuke thought that Dunston 'having made some steps on the road to improvement ... had become too much satisfied ... Mr. Dunston observed "you carry kind treatment at the Retreat too far" ' and expressed his belief that 'fear' was 'the most effectual principle by which to reduce the insane to orderly conduct'. Tuke naturally did not like this, nor the building which had 'entirely the appearance of a place of confinement'.

---

[1] Presumably *Hygëia: or essays moral and medical*, 1802–3, 3 volumes.
[2] Presumably the second edition of Thomas Arnold's *Observation on the nature, kinds, causes, and prevention of insanity*, 1806.

In June he started on the preface, but took three months to finish it; finally he put together the chapter 'Table and Statement of Cases'.

In March 1813 he sent the first part of his MS to the press, and on 8 May – when only 28 years old – he proudly 'Received from the printer a copy of my "Description of the Retreat". This work was commenced under a deep sense of the sufferings of the insane. Their afflictions have often been present with me in my retirement before God ... May He prosper this imperfect effort to awaken the public sympathy towards them!' HE did.

Tuke knew what he hoped to achieve: 'The great object of my publication was to furnish facts for those who were better able than myself to employ them for the general good. Benevolent persons in various places had long been dissatisfied with the system of management so generally pursued; but benevolent theory was powerless when opposed by practical experience' – that is until his book showed that it could be done. But he knew also the force of reaction:

> They who seek to change the most mischievous customs will find their most powerful opponents in those who boast the advantages of experience, and whose situations seemed to afford them the greatest right to decide as to the utility of change. Unhappily habit produces indifference to the most frightful evils. Indolence is stronger than feeling, and the voice of interest louder than that of reason.

The prospect of freeing the insane from neglect, maltreatment, chains and starvation found more ready echo in the hearts of social reformers and humanitarians than in the narrower views and vested interests of medical and non-medical madhouse keepers. The Reverend Sydney Smith, for instance, by this time installed at Heslington within a mile of the Retreat, wrote a handsome account of Tuke's book in his *Edinburgh Review* (1815, **23**, 189–98):

> The present account is given us by Mr. Tuke, a respectable tea-dealer in York ... The long account of the subscription at the beginning of the book, is evidently made tedious for the Quaker market; and Mr. Tuke is a little too much addicted to quoting. But, with these trifling exceptions, his book does him very great credit; – it is full of good sense and humanity, right feelings, and rational views. The Retreat for insane Quakers is situated about a mile from the city of York, upon an eminence commanding the adjacent country, and in the midst of a garden and fields belonging to the Institution. The great principle on which it appears to be conducted is that of kindness to the patients. It does not appear to them, because a man is mad upon one particular subject, that he is to be considered in a state of complete mental degradation, or insensible to the feelings of kindness and gratitude. When a madman does not do what he is bid to do, the shortest method, to be sure, is to knock him down; and straps and chains are the species of prohibitions which are the least frequently disregarded. But the society of Friends seems rather to consult the interest of the patient than the ease of his keeper; and to aim at the government of the insane, by creating in them the kindest disposition towards those who have the command over them. Nor can any thing be more

wise, humane, or interesting, than the strict attention to the feelings of their patients which seems to prevail.

He was confident that Tuke's work would 'gradually bring into repute a milder and better method of treating the insane'.

And such might have been the slow course of history had it not been greatly speeded up by the unexpected local opposition which the book aroused and the wide publicity the new methods gained in the ensuing strife. The affronted party was Tuke's neighbour, Dr. Charles Best, physician to York Lunatic Asylum. How Dr. Best, the accuser, became in turn the accused and how the discovery of terrible abuses at the Asylum led a band of philanthropists in London, inspired by the deeds of their Yorkshire friends, to investigate the conditions of the metropolitan asylums only to discover the grossest cruelties at Bethlem Hospital, and how these scandals led to the great Parliamentary Inquiry 1815-7 which laid the groundwork for the modern mental hospital era – all this makes an exciting chapter in the history of human institutions.

THE YORK LUNATIC ASYLUM

The York Asylum, designed for 54 patients, was one of a number of subscription hospitals for the insane which opened in the second half of the 18th century and owed their inspiration to the opening of St. Luke's Hospital in 1751. It was founded in 1772 and opened in September 1777 with Dr. Alexander Hunter,[1] its moving spirit, as physician. In *An earnest application to the humane public* (1777) for further funds to finish the building, he explained that it was urgently needed since 'no particular provision is made by law for Lunaticks, the common parish workhouses, and houses of correction, being no ways proper for their reception, either in point of accommodation, attendance, or medical assistance'. Besides there were 'only two general hospitals in this kingdom for the reception of Lunaticks', Bethlem and St. Luke's, both in London and 'the great expense attending the transportation of Lunatics' to them 'from the Northern parts of this Kingdom' and the uncertainty of getting them admitted made local provision essential. Furthermore, 'not the least consideration with the Promoters ... is the assistance that may be given to

[1] Alexander Hunter (1729–1809), M.D. EDIN., F.R.S. LOND. and EDIN., was a well known physician at York and a noted agriculturist and writer. Through his experience at York Asylum he became an authority on the building of 'Lunatic Hospitals'. Thomas Arnold consulted him when one was planned at Leicester, and Sir George O. Paul from Gloucester, whom he advised that 'An Asylum for Lunatics should always be a separate and independent charity; an union with an Infirmary is unnatural' (*Minutes of proceedings relative to the establishment of a general lunatic asylum, near the city of Glocester*, 1796). To James Currie of Liverpool he also expressed his preference for 'a distinct institution placed in the country though near the town'. It was probably due to Hunter more than anyone else that in the 19th century so many asylums came to be built in isolation away from general hospitals and from towns – a circumstance which contributed greatly to the isolation and retardation of psychiatry. Only now is this trend being actively reversed and a combination of general with mental hospitals again propagated. This is what Currie had maintained against Hunter's opinion in 1790 when a lunatic wing was added to the Liverpool Infirmary on the model of the Manchester Infirmary to which a Lunatic Hospital had been joined in 1766. It is interesting to note that by this development lunatic hospitals became lunatic asylums and that the return to combined hospitals in our time has brought back also the name of (mental) hospitals.

many persons of moderate circumstances, who, labouring under ... unsound mind, have no place to retire to but a private mad-house, where their cure stands a great chance of being protracted for the benefit of the mercenary keeper'.

In 1784 there was a change of system in the Asylum to allow admission of a number of patients 'of a superior or opulent class' at fees above the basic eight shillings per week, the excess to be used to reduce the charges for those who could not afford the minimum. Hunter, originally appointed without 'either fee or reward ... as long as the hospital continues to receive only paupers, or persons in low and indigent circumstances, agreeable to the original design of the charity', was consequently authorised in 1785 to take 'the reasonable emoluments of his profession' from patients who 'would *in another place* have been his own *private patients*'. When twenty years later the affairs of the Asylum were enquired into, it was found that this had opened the door to neglect of the pauper patients and misappropriation of funds, a fraud hidden from the Governors by the subterfuge of keeping a duplicate set of books, one open to inspection, the other giving the real takings and showing what had gone into the physician's pocket. A conservative estimate put the amount diverted from the charity at more than £20,000.

In 1788 some subscribers expressed alarm at seeing 'the Asylum ... converted from a public charity, into an hotel for the reception of persons of condition only' and at the ascendency of the physician over the Governors. They objected also to the system of charging parishes the full cost of maintenance while reducing payments for indigent patients not in receipt of parish relief, in consequence of which there were only six parish paupers in the house. To this reproach Hunter retorted that 'if the payments from the parish-poor should be reduced ... the house would be immediately, and most pressingly, filled with the lowest and meanest of the poor'.

In 1791 an incident occurred which, although 'apparently of a trivial nature was ... remarkable for the event to which it led ... a female of the Society of Friends was placed in the Asylum; and her family residing at a considerable distance, requested some of their acquaintance to visit her. These visits ... were refused on the ground of the patient not being in a suitable state to be seen by strangers – and, in a few weeks after her admission, death put a period to her sufferings. This ... first suggested to the Quakers the propriety of attempting an establishment for persons of their society' (see Note to page 22). Another attempt followed to force an enquiry at this time, but only resulted in Hunter strengthening his dominion further.

In December 1804 Hunter took Charles Best as his pupil, who was to succeed him both at the Asylum and in his private practice, and taught him to walk in his ways. To him he also disclosed 'the manner of preparing the different medicines, so successfully made use of ... of which the composition... [was]unknown to every person' but himself. These were of course the old 'insane powders' or 'antimaniacals', vomits, purges and diaphoretics, with which so much money had been made for centuries, by which so many had been duped and so many laid low. 'There is good reason to believe' wrote Samuel Tuke in 1846 in his *Review of the early history of the Retreat* 'that the medical practice, in this institution, consisted ... in the routine administration of drastic aperients and emetics, in the form of green and grey powders; and – that the benefit of these means might not be confined to the inmates of the Asylum – the nostrums of the physician, as of sovereign remedy to cure the distempered brain, were sold by his agent in the city, and through him, in a great part of Yorkshire and the North of England'. Naturally 'the founders of the Retreat, despising pretence, and of great decision of character' when the time came 'declined the proffered services of the experienced visiting physician of the Asylum' and instead appointed Dr. Thomas Fowler 'who was not likely to walk idly in the steps of authority, and who had already, by his investigations, done something to promote the true honour of medical art ' (see Note to page xi).

When Hunter died in 1809 some friends of the Asylum agitated once more for a change of system. A pamphlet appeared entitled *Observations on the present state of the York Lunatic Asylum*, supported by an open letter from William Tuke to the Governors from which the following is an extract:

> I have long been apprehensive that there is room for some improvement in the general plan of managing the York Asylum. The physician who had, not only the medical care, but nearly the sole government of the institution, being deceased, it now appears necessary for the Governors to pause awhile, and maturely consider, previous to another appointment, whether a different mode of government may not conduce to the benevolent purposes for which it was established. Should it be admitted that some improvements may be made by new institutions from observing the defects of those which are of older date, I hope to be excused for taking the liberty of submitting to the Governors of the Asylum some remarks at the present crisis ... It is generally known that I have taken a very active part in the establishment of a similar institution, called the Retreat ... and as it has succeeded far beyond my expectation, I feel a wish to contribute such information as attentive observation may enable me, for the benefit of others.

He pointed out that the original purpose to benefit the insane poor had been lost sight of; that the admission of patients was open to abuse; that the accounts and funds were in a state of confusion if not worse; that the medical practice had been too long kept secret; and that a milder system of management should now be adopted. He quoted 'with much satisfaction' the remarks of Lord Chancellor Erskine on the treatment of the insane, which his Lordship had 'found so generally severe, that in case they were but a little deranged, it was sufficient to make them raving mad: and he delivered it as his judgment, that kind and conciliating treatment was the best means to promote recovery. The latter part of this opinion, I have the satisfaction of asserting' added grandfather Tuke with pardonable pride, 'has been evidently proved correct in the management of the Retreat'.

Despite these appeals Best was appointed and carried on his master's tradition unmolested. He even managed early in 1813 to get the Governors to resolve 'that no persons unconnected with the Asylum shall have the liberty of visiting any of the patients without a printed order of admission, signed by the Physician'. In plain words he 'had now obtained an absolute dominion; everything was under his sole control. At no period had a change in the management seemed more hopeless ... Every avenue to reform ... seemed ... closed'.

At this juncture the *Description of the Retreat* appeared. Although revolutionary in spirit, it did not directly attack any other system or institution – albeit that by introducing 'mild' treatment specifically so named, the old system by contrast was branded as 'terrific'. The physician of the Asylum, sensing danger, took offence at the mention of the historical fact that the Retreat owed its origin to the dissatisfaction of the Friends with the treatment of one of their members 'in a neighbouring institution'; and he felt threatened by the reflection cast on the methods of the Asylum by the moral treatment pioneered at the Retreat. Believing attack to be his best method of defence, he published a protest in the *York Chronicle* of September signed 'Evigilator' which set in train the events which finally hoisted him with his own petard:

> When an attempt is made to injure the reputation and interests of any public body, or private individual, it is of little moment to the assailed party, whether the measure be accomplished by open libel or masked insinuation ... In an account of the Quakers' Retreat ... some highly indecorous and injurious insinuations were thrown out against other Establishments ... the intended application of which no one could misunderstand.

He went on to complain that a handbill had been circulated advertising the private asylum of the physician of the Retreat, Dr. Belcombe, at Clifton, stating that it was conducted 'with a view to introduce on a small scale, the mild methods of treatments in use at that institution'–'It would be an act of culpable supineness' exclaimed Best 'to allow it to pass by ... It must be obvious to everyone, that the words ... were intended to impose a belief on its readers, that methods of treatment of an opposite description, were employed at the other Establishments for insane persons in York and its Vicinity'. Clearly he was as concerned to protect the fair name of his own private asylum at Acomb–erstwhile Hunter's House of Retirement–as with any slur on the Asylum.

Samuel Tuke defended himself and his book in the *Chronicle* of the following week: 'It was neither affirmed nor insinuated in the work which has given so much offense, that bad practices exist in all establishments... Whence, then, has arisen this extreme tenderness in the mind of "Evigilator" '. But he hastened to add 'If anything which is said in the "Description of the Retreat" is calculated to *sap* or *undermine* that detestable system of treatment to which the insane are too frequently exposed, I shall sincerely rejoice'. Best countered by declaring that to speak of 'the practicability of introducing a system of mild treatment' generally into asylums was tantamount to 'a direct assertion that such a system had not been introduced into *any* establishment of the kind – a sufficient proof that it was the author's intention to include a neighbouring institution in his sweeping censure'. Tuke answered once more in the *Chronicle* of 14 October, quoting Dr. Andrew Duncan senior's tribute to the achievements of the Retreat.[1] At this stage Lindley Murray (see Note to page 24) advised Tuke to let the matter rest, but another friend, Thomas Wemyss, took up the cudgels and published a letter supporting him signed 'Civis', to which 'A Governor of the Asylum' and 'Irrisor' replied. These in turn provoked an answer from Samuel's father Henry signed 'Non-Irrisor'.

Just when this paper war seemed to be petering out, the affair took an unexpected and, in the event, decisive turn by the advent on the scene of Godfrey Higgins,[2] justice of the peace of Skellow Grange near Doncaster. He had been applied to in April for a warrant to apprehend one William Vickers who had assaulted an old woman, but finding him insane, sent him to York Asylum despite Mrs. Vickers' protest that her husband 'would be ill treated there'. But, wrote Higgins later regretfully 'I paid no attention to her fears ... I heard no more about the poor man until October, when she came to me to ask for relief, and complained that her husband had been ill used in the Asylum'. A surgeon found 'he had the itch very bad, was extremely filthy ... his health so much impaired, that he was not able to stand by himself; his legs were very much swelled, and one of them in a state of mortification' – evidence of the use of chains and starvation. Finding 'a general belief prevalent ... that great abuses did exist in the York Asylum' Higgins decided to force 'a general inquiry into the actual state of the charity'.

When Best got wind of this he at once convened a special meeting of Governors to investigate. But Higgins, determined that the matter should not be hushed up as others had been in the Asylum's history, published the facts in the York and Doncaster newspapers. Grandfather Tuke seized the opportunity to throw his weight behind Higgins and in a public letter expressed the earnest hope that there would be a full attendance of Governors to whom he submitted for their 'serious consideration' a selection of 'judicious regulations for the prevention and detection of abuses, in a class of institutions of all others the most exposed to them'. In the mean-

---

[1] This is reprinted at page 226 of the *Description* from *Short account of the rise, progress, and present state of the Lunatic Asylum at Edinburgh, with some remarks on the general treatment of lunatics, pointing out the advantages of avoiding all severity*, Edinburgh 1812.

[2] Godfrey Higgins (1773–1833), archaeologist and county magistrate of the West Riding. After the episode recorded here he visited Pinel in Paris, persuaded his fellow justices to establish the West Riding Asylum at Wakefield, and sponsored the appointment of Dr. (later Sir) William Charles Ellis as its first director.

time Higgins had continued his inquiries and collected more cases of mal-treatment and these he also forwarded to the Governors.

At the special Court which met on 2 December 1813 'Mr. Higgins's statement was read; after which, the accused servants of the house were called in and ... denied upon oath, the truth of the charges. No other evidence was called' and the Governors passed a resolution, directed to be advertised in the newspapers, that they were 'unanimously of opinion that during the time that the said William Vickers remained in the Asylum he was treated with all care, attention, and humanity'. The Court then adjourned to consider Higgins's other cases the following week.

Samuel Tuke was so incensed that he sent a letter to the *York Courant* signed 'A Hater of Abuses':

> I cannot refrain from wishing to call the attention of your readers ... to the decision of the Quarterly Court of Governors of the York Lunatic Asylum ... It is stated ... that such witnesses were examined upon oath ... as were competent to give information. Will the public believe that these competent witnesses were no others than the managers and keepers of that Asylum? ... Is it possible that upon the mere denial of guilt by the parties accused, the Governors have formed their opinion ... There are four other cases of complaint, yet unnoticed by the Court ... Let them not, therefore, imagine that the whole business is decided ...

Higgins equally disgusted and worried about what was going on be-hind the Asylum wall, now joined forces with the Tukes. His correspon-dence with Samuel was described, seventy years later, as a 'mass of private letters' showing 'their combined endeavours (under the fiercest opposi-tion) to reform the horrible abuses which had converted a well-inten-tioned charity into a hell upon earth'. 'Our new ally' wrote Samuel to his cousin William Maud on 30 November 'has come forward most oppor-tunely. He is furnished with other cases besides the one which is pub-lished'.

At this crucial moment they were joined by Samuel William Nicoll, barrister-at-law[1] whose entry was as dramatic as his wit subtle and his judgement fair. When the adjourned Court of Governors met on 10 December to consider Higgin's remaining allegations of cruelty and neglect, they were amazed to find thirteen new faces present.

> On that day Mr. Nicoll and twelve other persons went down to the Asylum, at the hour of the meeting, and paid the requisite donations [£20 each] to become Governors. After some hesitation as to the point of regularity ... they were ad-mitted ... It would be difficult to conceive the surprise occasioned by this unex-pected incursion ... Considerable indignation was naturally felt and expressed; but the impartial and dignified conduct of the chairman (the Archbishop of York) contributed to restrain the meeting within the bounds of decorum

– wrote Jonathan Gray, historian of, and himself an actor in this episode

---

1 S. W. Nicoll (1769–1833), counsel to the corporation of the city of York, Recorder of Doncaster (1807 and York (1829). Author of *An enquiry into the present state of visitation in asylums for the reception of the insane; and into the modes, by which such visitation may be improved*, 1828 (see Plate 2 (c)).

and one of that gallant band of new Governors which included the van-
guard of the Tukes, Samuel's cousin Daniel.

The new Governors forebore to propose any revision of the decision in
the case of Vickers

> 'or even to allude to it, conceiving that this would be an unnecessary attack ...
> on those with whom they were now to be associated. They were persuaded, that out
> of Mr. Higgins's remaining cases, if properly investigated, enough would be proved
> to evince the necessity of a change of system. On the first of these cases, therefore,
> being brought forward, Mr. Nicoll proposed, that instead of an inquiry by the
> whole court, a *Committee of investigation* should be appointed. Mr. Nicoll's proposal
> was violently opposed – there were only "a couple of lousy cases, which might be
> disposed of in half an hour". The Archbishop, however, declared himself so
> decidedly in favour of a Committee ... that the opposition to it was withdrawn
> ... Mr. Nicoll next proposed, that the Committee should inquire *generally* into
> the *rules* and *management* of the institution, but withdrew the motion on the
> Archbishop 'promising to second it at a future meeting if sufficient grounds should
> have been established'.

The Committee of nine which included the Archbishop, the Lord
Mayor, Nicoll and Gray met five times between 20 and 27 December. On
the following evening, while Nicoll was dining with Tuke at Mrs. Cappe's
(see Note to page 61), fire broke out at the Asylum and destroyed the
detached wing. 'A most alarming fire broke out ... in the north-west
building of the Asylum where there were about sixty men and twenty five
women confined' wrote Tuke in his diary, 'the origin of the fire is not
known. But it was first observed in a room in which flocks were kept, and
to which it is said no person had been that day. The flames made very
rapid progress, and at ten o'clock nearly the whole of the building was
consumed. Happily a favourable state of the wind, and the water supplied
by the engines, prevented communication with the centre or any other
buildings'. The next morning he inspected 'the ruins': 'The walls and
chimneys are left standing. There are said to be six patients missing, of
whom it is said four have perished in the flames. The other two, it is supposed, have escaped'.

The disaster occurring at this very moment gave rise to the grave suspicion of arson to destroy incriminating evidence. 'Notwithstanding the
slight and desultory inquiry which took place ... I have never been able
to divest my mind of suspicions of the most horrible kind respecting its
cause' wrote Higgins two years later. The physician was away that night,
the Apothecary and Matron (Mr. and Mrs. Atkinson) were out and so
were all the other servants but two, one of whom was incapacitated by
asthma and old age. The Steward, aged 82, barred the gate against
willing helpers 'fearing lest the Asylum be plundered'.

Samuel Tuke and William Maud waited on the Governors to offer
shelter for patients from the destroyed buildings: 'We were introduced ...
The Archbishop rose and ... expressed warmly the thanks of the Gover-

nors, but stated that, on the representation of Dr. Best, it appeared that the house would be able to accommodate all the patients; but that if further inquiry should lead to a different opinion, the Governors would thankfully accept the offer of the Retreat'. Incidentally, a similar offer came from Nottingham Asylum, opened 1811, the first county asylum established under Wynn's Act.

Meanwhile Best's campaign against the Retreat and Higgins continued unabated. A letter signed 'A Friend to Truth' appeared in the *Courant* 'making' – Samuel noted in his diary – 'false statements in regard to the number of patients in the Asylum and inferring from them that the proportion of deaths in the Retreat was greater than those in the Asylum. I examined the printed annual reports [of the Asylum] from the commencement ... and found all the data, and consequently the inferences, entirely unfounded'. He answered this renewed attack point for point in the *Chronicle* over the signature 'A Seeker of Truth' concluding that 'Whatever friendship this writer may have for truth, he has a most unhappy way of shewing it'. Indeed so false were the figures that when Higgins later examined the Asylum books he found that whereas 365 patients had actually died, only 221 had so been entered, while of the remaining 144, 101 were entered 'discharged cured'.

The reformers now mounted their major offensive. Having once before successfully gate-crashed the Governors' Court, they now invaded it in overwhelming numbers. At the adjourned Court on 7 January 1814 which was to deal with the report on Higgins's remaining cases, another batch of twenty-seven turned up, paid the requisite donation, and were enrolled as Governors, among them Godfrey Higgins; and William and Samuel Tuke who were tauntingly told that although their donations made them Governors they 'did not make them gentlemen'. Of the sixty Governors present, no less than forty were of the reformers' contingent. Between them they had paid £800.

'My grandfather and myself having qualified ourselves as Governors' wrote Samuel that evening 'attended the adjourned meeting of the Governors at the Asylum. The Archbishop was in the chair. He opened the business by a most able, humane and candid speech, in which he confessed the change which had taken place in his sentiments in regard to the state of the Asylum, by an investigation of the cases of complaint. He showed the extraordinary care necessary to guard against abuses in this class of institutions, and expressed in high terms his satisfaction with the conduct of his colleagues on the committee. Their report stated, that in one of the cases –that of Kidd [Martha Kidd, admitted September 1806 and removed to Pontefract Poorhouse in October 1812] –gross neglect of personal cleanliness was in full proof; that in the case of Schorey [the Reverend John Butterfield Schorey, formerly of Queen's College, Oxford, who was in the asylum on three occasions from 1807 and died there in December 1812], it appeared evident that there had been neglect of cleanliness; and that the conduct of several of the attendants had been highly reprehensible. The charges in the other cases were not sufficiently established to require censure. Their report was adopted as the act of the meeting; and it was also resolved that a committee be appointed to examine into the rules, management, and state of the Asylum, to report facts and their opinions thereon at a future meeting ... The decided numerical superiority of the reformers ... who had entered for the sole purpose of benefiting the charity by restoring it to its original intention, and by the institution of such guards against abuses as are most likely to prevent them' added Samuel with some relief, 'prevented any attempt at opposition and thus resolutions, which three months ago would have been spurned with disdain, were carried unanimously'. To mark the occasion he sent the Archbishop a copy of his *Description of the Retreat*.

One week later the Tukes made their first tour of the Asylum as Governors:

> The number [of patients] at this time is about 160, who are all in the principal building and are of course extremely crowded. Upwards of twenty patients were shut up together in very small day-rooms which had not convenience for air, exercise or natural wants. The appearance of the men was pitiable beyond description. Most of their faces were very hollow, and their complexion sallow. Their noses generally had that red or livid appearance which marks penury and neglect, and the closeness of the rooms was almost intolerable.

Samuel saw one patient 'without any clothes whatever, standing in a wash-house on a wet stone floor apparently in the last stage of decay. The condition of the patient's body was filthy in the extreme ... He was spoken of by all as a dying man'. At his insistence 'he was removed to another part of the asylum, where he was better attended, and in a few months was so much recovered as to be removed to his parish in an inoffensive though imbecile state of mind'.

They followed this by taking a party of new Governors including Nicoll round the Retreat to show them what could be done. Yet Samuel was far from complacent about their achievement – 'the Retreat has several considerable defects' he confided to his diary and went on to consider them under three headings. First, the buildings did not sufficiently allow for the surveillance of patients; he would have preferred the panopticon plan of Jeremy Bentham used in the planning of the Glasgow Asylum by William Stark (see Note to page 106). He also wondered whether 'the height of the walls might not be dispensed with'. Second, 'the system of management' could be improved by paying more attention to the classification of patients 'according to their states of mind'. He regretted that the nurses were 'so fully employed in acts of real service to the patients, that they have not sufficient time to endeavour to amuse them by walks, &c. ... One person ... possessing intelligence and humanity might be extremely useful in paying a general attention to the patients, and sitting with such as are most convalescent and rational'. Third, he felt

that the rules of the Retreat should provide for still more frequent visitation – the surest way of preventing abuses – a subject to which Nicoll later
devoted a small treatise (see Plate 2 (c)). How desirable these improvements are in many institutions even today!

At the end of February Tuke was able to report to William Maud that

the Asylum business is going on very well, but we know not what opposition
we may meet with at the General Meeting in the Eighth Month when every thing
will have to be decided. If ... any of your neighbours are thinking of becoming
Governors, I wish they would enter soon ... Many old Governors, who, we hear,
may have some attachment to the old ways, will probably attend the meeting and
if Dr. Best's friends mean to make any effort, then must be their time. The further
the Committee proceed in their investigation, the more is the whole system and
practice proved iniquitous. It now plainly appears to be a mere private job prepared at the public expense for the benefit of the physician ... those patients who
pay above fourteen shillings per week, are considered as under the private care
of Dr. Best and he puts in his pocket all that is paid by them above that sum.

But still worse was to come. The indefatigable Higgins continued to
'entertain grave suspicion that very gross abuses still prevailed' and when
he found himself in York in 'assize week ... to attend on the grand jury'
he determined to inspect every inch of the Asylum himself. This he did at
eight o'clock on the morning of 24 March 1814. What he saw is best told
as he described it to the Parliamentary Committee which very properly
opened its proceedings the following year with his evidence:

I went early in the morning to examine every place; after ordering a great
number of doors to be opened, I came to one which was in a retired situation in
the kitchen apartments, and which was almost hid by the opening of a door in the
passage; I ordered this door to be opened; the keepers hesitated, and said ... they
had not the key; I ordered them to get the key, but it was said to be mislaid, and
not to be found at the moment; upon this I grew angry, and told them ... that if
they would not find it, I could find a key at the kitchen fire-side, namely the poker;
upon that the key was immediately brought. When the door was opened, I went
into the passage, and I found four cells, I think of about eight feet square, in a very
horrid and filthy situation, the straw appeared almost saturated with urine and
... the walls were daubed with excrement. The air holes ... in each cell, were
partly filled with it ... I asked the keeper, if these cells were inhabited by the
patients? and was told they were at night. I then desired him to take me up stairs,
and shew me the place of the women, who came out of these cells that morning ...
he shewed me into a room ... the size of which he told me was twelve feet by seven
feet ten inches, and in which there were thirteen women, who he told me had all
come out of these cells that morning ... I became very sick, and could not remain
longer in the room ... Before I saw these cells I had been repeatedly told by Atkinson, the Apothecary, and the keepers, that I had seen the whole house that was
occupied by the patients – as indeed had the Archbishop and other Governors
since inquiries started, none of whom knew of the existence of these cells.

At the Quarterly Court on 14 April this new scandal caused much
'violent altercation and recrimination' and despite opposition from the

old Governors who shielded Best, Nicoll's motion was carried 'that it is the opinion of this Court that Mr. Higgins is entitled to the thanks of the Governors for his upright, persevering and successful exertions in bringing to light the abuses which have prevailed in this institution'. At this Court also, and for the first time for more than a quarter of a century, visitors were appointed to ensure that such things could never happen again.

Although the road now seemed clear, Higgins took the precaution to publish in the newspapers just before the crucial annual general meeting on 26 August a re-statement of the ill-fated history of the Asylum, ending with this appeal to the Governors:

> In the name of all those persons, whose violent deaths are so stated in your books as to disguise the facts from you, I call for justice. In the name of one hundred and forty four patients whose deaths have been concealed from the Public and from you, I call for justice. I call upon you to clear the house of every individual, who has neglected or abused his authority. I call upon you to cleanse the Augean stable from top to bottom.

The Meeting was held at Guildhall under the chairmanship of the Archbishop of York and lasted two days. Samuel Tuke recorded it as follows:

> A new code of rules, which had previously passed the committee and the Governors' Court, were discussed, and, with some amendments, passed. Lord Fitzwilliam and Lord Milton expressed the greatest surprise at the misapplication of the funds, and questioned Dr. B. in a very severe manner. He had, however, a numerous host of friends; and it seemed in vain to attempt to obtain that justice in his case which could be procured in regard to the inferior officers. A resolution was proposed for the re-election of all the officers of the institution, – *i.e.* that all the places should be declared vacant on a certain day ... and ... was agreed ... The responsibility of Dr. B. for the maltreatment of the patients was not inquired into. His examination was solely confined to misapplication of funds. There were about eighty Governors present.

In other words every resident officer, keeper and nurse was discharged, Dr. Best being allowed to resign on the grounds of ill-health. The steward – as if to set the seal on this infamous episode and to justify the reformers – refused to hand over the books in his charge. Instead he burnt them and so for ever destroyed the true record of the Asylum's patients and funds.

Total victory had been achieved. Not only had the spirit of the Retreat triumphed over the Asylum, but its very officers took over the running of it: George and Katherine Jepson reformed its internal management and superintended the patients until the new staff arrived; Samuel and cousin Daniel along with Nicoll, Gray and others 'were appointed a committee of management, according to the new rules. Three ladies were appointed weekly visitors; James Richardson, John Mason, William Tuke, and C. Wellbeloved, the visitors for the quarter'.

'What strenuous efforts fruitlessly combined to accomplish, a little volume in which the Asylum was scarcely mentioned, has at once achieved – I hardly need name Mr. S. Tuke's ... "Description of the Retreat" ', wrote Nicoll, the third of the victorious triumvirate: Tuke the tireless humanitarian whose motto was that nothing has been done while anything remains undone; the hot-headed Higgins who ruthlessly exposed the evils; and Nicoll himself whose cool legal brain devised the strategy.

BETHLEM HOSPITAL

It was not to be supposed that the campaign to liberalise and humanise the treatment of the insane would long remain a local matter. The experiment of the Retreat was an expression of the new attitude to the welfare of the underprivileged in an age when all the old tyrannies were assailed – of social order, of religion, of slavery – and found a ready echo in the minds of progressive men in the metropolis. Among these Edward Wakefield (1774–1854), land-agent of Pall Mall was a leading figure. In 1812 he had already put forward a plan for the establishment of public asylums for the insane in *The Philanthropist*, followed in 1813 by a renewed appeal in the same periodical. In this he reprinted the evidence of Sir George O. Paul before the *Select Committee*, 1807 which led to the passing of the *Act for better Care and Maintenance of Lunatics, being Paupers or Criminals in England*, 1808, known as Wynn's Act. Even if Tuke's *Description of the Retreat* had not further fired his zeal, its review in *The Philanthropist* (1813, **3**, 326–38) certainly did so. It was written by Thomas Hancock (1783–1848), M.D. EDIN., L.R.C.P., physician to the City and Finsbury Dispensaries, Quaker school fellow of Samuel Tuke, with whom he had corresponded as early as 1804 on 'the subject of insanity':

> It is curious to observe by what slow degree the reign of terror and oppression has been retiring from various conditions of civilised man ... Can it be necessary to recur to the long experience of so many thousand years, before we can see the maxim generally established and practically observed – that mild institutions will produce more immediate and decisive benefits ... than the exercise of severe laws? ... The treatment of those whose minds have suffered a transient lapse from the dominion of reason, has of late years ... undergone a change no less salutary to the objects themselves than favourable to the interests of humanity ... Whoever is acquainted with the modes formerly in use ... will be willing to offer his sincere acknowledgements to the author of the work before us, for presenting to the world a proof so clear and decisive of the superior excellence of a system of management founded upon principles so consistent with humanity as those established at the York Retreat ... How unlike to that inhuman system, partaking more of a vindictive than sanative complexion, under which the unhappy lunatic was tortured with stripes and blows and chains, till his diseased passions were fired with a degree of fury and indignation unquenchable and unappeasable.

Wakefield gathered a committee to found a 'London Asylum' to be run on Retreat lines. It was announced in *The Medical and Physical Journal*, April 1814 in an editorial note by Dr. Samuel Fothergill, nephew of the great Quaker Dr. John: 'Among the projected institutions of these

improving times, we observe a plan for establishing an asylum for lunatics in or near the metropolis' in which 'humanity ... is to form a leading
principle in the treatment of patients'.

His committee first studied the existing establishments and visited the
lunatic wards at Guy's, St. Luke's and Bethlem. It was at Bethlem, the
oldest surviving foundation for the insane in England, a Royal Hospital
given to the city of London by Henry VIII, that they discovered the grossest ill-treatment equal to if not worse than anything brought to light at
York. 'There seems but one alternative in the care of maniacs–occasional accidents, or perpetual restraint ... In the York Asylum, there is
the strongest evidence of whatever gross neglect could produce–but
Bethlem Hospital exhibits a cold premeditated system, in which coercion is to supersede the necessity of habitual care', wrote an anonymous
contemporary.

As at York they had difficulty in gaining access. At their first visit they
were chaperoned by a Governor who was so overpowered by what he
saw that it had to be broken off. They renewed their attempt on 2 May
and what they found may be said–like Higgins's visitation at York
Asylum hardly six weeks before–to have made history. Only a brief extract from Wakefield's committee's report can be given here as sum-
marised in *The Medical and Physical Journal* for August 1814:

> One of the side rooms contained about ten [female] patients, each chained by
> one arm to the wall; the chain allowing them merely to stand up by the bench or
> form fixed to the wall, or to sit down on it. The nakedness of each patient was
> covered by a blanket-gown only ... Many other unfortunate women were locked
> up in their cells, naked, and chained on straw ... In the men's wing, in the side
> room, six patients were chained close to the wall by the right arm as well as by
> the right leg ... Their nakedness and their mode of confinement gave this room
> the complete appearance of a dog-kennel.

But a still more horrific example of man's inhumanity to mad humanity faced them when they found William Norris in solitary confinement
in perhaps the most vicious restraining apparatus ever devised. So incred-
ible was the sight that, as Wakefield explained to the Parliamentary
Committee the following year, he had not only taken the precaution of
bringing members of Parliament to see for themselves (among them
Thomas Thompson, M.P. for Hull, a Governor of York Asylum and
friend of Higgins and Ellis), but had also brought an artist to make a
permanent pictorial record on the spot (see Plate 1 (a)).

Their visit had indeed furnished them with 'the strongest grounds for
recommending a new asylum, to be conducted after the simple and mild
... plan of the "Friends' Retreat" '. But in the end they achieved so much
more that their planned asylum became unnecessary (although details
of it with plans and elevation appear in the 1815 Report). They had provided that redoubtable champion of lunacy reform the Honourable
George Rose, M.P. (1744–1818), whose bills had repeatedly failed to pass

THE INFLUENCE OF THE RETREAT IN AMERICA 19

one or other House, with the incontestable evidence he needed to force an enquiry into the whole field of provision for, and supervision of the insane in England, Scotland and Ireland. Under his chairmanship a Parliamentary Committee started sitting in May 1815 and its reports and appendices which make up 450 folio pages remain a monumental documentary on every aspect of how asylums were managed and patients treated. Great improvements followed through what Nicoll called the 'visitation of the public' even before the enactment of new legislation in 1828.

How fitting that William Tuke who conceived and nursed the Retreat and who for years had been its 'Manager-in-Chief', who 'regularly conducted the affairs of the institution till the decay of his sight obliged him, in his 88th year, to close his long and gratuitous services', should be invited to London to place his experience before the Committee. Asked from the chair by Rose 'Is the statement published by Mr. Samuel Tuke ... a correct statement of the mode of treating patients at the York Retreat?' he answered simply 'I had the revision of it before it went to the press, and I know it to be perfectly correct'.

Thus what had started as a local, private, sectarian experiment in charity wrought a fundamental change in the attitude to the insane in England and spread throughout the civilised world.

THE INFLUENCE OF THE RETREAT IN AMERICA

Outside England the *Description of the Retreat* made its most immediate impact on America, where all the asylums established in the years following – Frankford, McLean, Bloomingdale and the Hartford Retreat – were patterned on the lines described by Tuke. This was due to the close link between the English and American Friends who were responsible for an American edition which appeared in Philadelphia 1813, and in the following year for an epitome in *Account of the rise and progress of the asylum, proposed to be established [at Frankford], near Philadelphia, for the relief of persons deprived of the use of their reason. With an abridged account of the Retreat, a similar institution near York, in England,* Philadelphia 1814. In 1815 Tuke wrote *A letter on pauper lunatic asylums* for the guidance of Thomas Eddy of New York who was advocating the establishment of a country branch of the New York Hospital 'for the moral treatment of the insane' on the lines of the Retreat (opened 1821 as Bloomingdale Asylum). Tuke's letter was published at the request of the governors of the hospital (New York 1815) and reprinted in *A psychiatric milestone* (New York 1921), the Bloomingdale Hospital Centenary volume.

The distinguished American psychiatrist Pliny Earle, then superintendent of Bloomingdale, who visited the Retreat during a tour of European asylums in 1837, wrote:

It is probable that no other man living, without the pale of the medical profession, is so well acquainted with the proper management of the insane, and the

most suitable construction, arrangement and discipline of lunatic asylums ...
'The Retreat near York' has long been quoted in the United States, as approaching nearer to perfection in its management, and as giving a higher per centage of
cures than any other establishment (*A visit to thirteen asylums in Europe*, Philadelphia 1839).

WAKEFIELD – HANWELL – DR. W. C. ELLIS

The events at York led Higgins to persuade his fellow magistrates of
the West Riding to build an asylum under their own control. They advertised liberal premiums for the best designs and invited Samuel Tuke
to draw up a set of basic requirements for the guidance of competitors.
In amplification of these instructions Tuke wrote his *Practical hints on the
construction and economy of pauper lunatic asylums*, York 1815, a small book of
55 pages 'intended to exhibit the rationale of the instructions ... for the
architects' (see Plate 2 (*a*)). A 'new and enlarged edition' appeared in the
prize winners' Messrs. Watson & Pritchett's elephant folio *Plans, eleva-
tions, sections, and description of the Pauper Lunatic Asylum, lately erected at
Wakefield, for the West-Riding of Yorkshire*, York 1819.

Thirteen years later Tuke was again consulted officially about new
asylums, this time not only in England and America but also in Europe.
In May 1828 he noted in his diary 'My leisure has been very much occu-
pied with Asylum matters, in conferring with persons relative to the
Middlesex, Geneva and Petersburgh buildings'. From Geneva his assis-
tance had been enlisted by the son of Dr. de la Rive who had visited the
Retreat in 1798 and had written a glowing account of it in *Bibliothèque
Britannique*. The enquiry from St. Petersburgh doubtless came from the
Emperor of Russia via Sir Alexander Crichton who in 1816 as 'the Grand
Duke Nicholas and Dr. Crichton' had visited the Retreat when Tuke had
presented them with copies of both his books, hoping thereby to make the
visit 'useful to the unhappy maniacs of the great empire Russia'.

The county of Middlesex had determined to build an asylum 'under
Wynn's Act' following the *Report from the Select Committee on Pauper Lunatics
in the County of Middlesex, and on Lunatic Asylums*, 1828 and like the magistrates of the West Riding had advertised a public competition. William
Alderson, architect of the Friends' Meeting House at Stoke Newington
took his plans to Samuel Tuke whose many suggestions led him to make
'a wholly fresh design' which won the prize. This asylum opened at Hanwell in 1831 with Ellis as medical superintendent (Higgins acted as
surety for him in the sum of £1,000) and became the scene of Conolly's
great reforms from 1839.

To return to Wakefield Asylum. In his preface to *Practical hints* Tuke
drew attention to the stimulating effect of advances in treatment on
asylum construction, and how better buildings induced better care:

> The public are greatly indebted to the visiting magistrates of the proposed
> Wakefield Asylum, for the attention and competition excited by their widely dif-
> fused invitation for plans and the liberal premiums offered for three of the most

STATE

OF AN

INSTITUTION

NEAR

YORK,

CALLED

THE RETREAT,

FOR PERSONS AFFLICTED

WITH

DISORDERS OF THE MIND.

———

YORK:

PRINTED BY W. BLANCHARD AND SON.

———

1815.

(b)

(a)

Plate 1

(a)

PRACTICAL HINTS

ON THE

CONSTRUCTION AND ECONOMY

OF

Pauper Lunatic Asylums;

INCLUDING INSTRUCTIONS TO THE ARCHITECTS WHO OFFERED
PLANS FOR THE

WAKEFIELD ASYLUM,

AND A SKETCH OF THE MOST APPROVED DESIGN.

By SAMUEL TUKE.

York:

PRINTED FOR WILLIAM ALEXANDER, AND SOLD BY HIM;
ALSO BY DARTON AND CO.; WM. PHILLIPS; AND LONGMAN, HURST
AND CO. LONDON.

1815.

(a)

(b)

A

LETTER

TO

THOMAS THOMPSON, Esq. M. P.

CONTAINING

CONSIDERATIONS ON THE NECESSITY OF PROPER PLACES BEING
PROVIDED BY THE LEGISLATURE

FOR THE RECEPTION OF ALL

INSANE PERSONS,

AND ON SOME OF THE ABUSES WHICH HAVE BEEN
FOUND TO EXIST IN MADHOUSES;

WITH

A PLAN TO REMEDY THEM.

BY W. C. ELLIS,

MEMBER OF THE ROYAL COLLEGE OF SURGEONS.

HULL:

PRINTED BY TOPPING AND DAWSON.

SOLD BY LONGMAN, HURST, REES, ORME, AND BROWN;
AND BALDWIN, CRADOCK, AND JOY, LONDON.

1815.

(b)

(c)

AN ENQUIRY

INTO THE

PRESENT STATE OF VISITATION,

IN

ASYLUMS

FOR THE

RECEPTION OF THE INSANE;

AND INTO THE MODES

BY WHICH SUCH VISITATION MAY BE IMPROVED.

BY S. W. NICOLL.

LONDON:

PRINTED FOR HARVEY AND DARTON,
55, GRACECHURCH-STREET,

1828.

(c)

(d)

ON THE

CONSTRUCTION AND MANAGEMENT

OF

HOSPITALS FOR THE INSANE;

WITH A PARTICULAR NOTICE OF

THE INSTITUTION AT SIEGBURG.

BY Dr. MAXIMILIAN JACOBI.

TRANSLATED BY JOHN KITCHING.

WITH

INTRODUCTORY OBSERVATIONS, &c.,

BY SAMUEL TUKE.

LONDON:

JOHN CHURCHILL, PRINCES STREET, SOHO;
J. L. LINNEY, YORK.
1841.

(d)

Plate 2

approved. The talent displayed in many of the numerous designs, which were, in consequence, presented by Architects from every part of the kingdom [forty plans were submitted], and the practical inquiry into the actual wants of Asylums, evinced in several of their descriptions, proves the readiness of the profession to second the enlightened views of the present time in regard to the treatment of the insane ... Chains, which seemed to identify the madman and the felon, are discarded from some of the largest establishments; and maniacs, who for many years were manacled with irons, are on a sudden, under a more mild and vigilant system of management, found to be gentle and inoffensive. But though much has been done—much still remains to be effected ... At a time, therefore, when so many Asylums are erecting, it seems incumbent on those, whose duty or inclination leads them to observe the wants of insane persons, and the defects of the older erections, to point them out for general consideration.

It opened in 1818 with Ellis in charge. He was well acquainted with the work of the Tukes and, in the neighbouring city of Hull, had founded in 1814, and ran with Dr. John Alderson, the Refuge for the Insane on the lines of the Retreat. In his *Letter to Thomas Thompson, Esq.* M.P., Hull 1815 (see Plate 2 (*b*)) which prepared the way for his appointment, he stressed the need for public asylums (Higgins had told him there were in the West Riding 600 insane paupers without provision), moral treatment and the necessity of vigilant inspection, quoting much from both Tuke's books. Later Ellis became famous for his policy of employing patients in purposive occupations both at Wakefield and Hanwell, and Tuke paid him handsome albeit posthumous tribute in his introduction to the English translation of Maximilian Jacobi's[1] *On the construction and management of hospitals for the insane*, 1841 (see Plate 2 (*d*)):

> In turning to the subject of labour in connexion with the management of the insane, it is due to the memory of the late Sir William Ellis, to bear in mind, that to him we are indebted for the first extensive and successful experiment to introduce labour systematically into our public asylums. He carried it out at Wakefield with a skill, vigour, and kindliness towards the patients, which were alike creditable to his understanding and his heart. He first proved, that there was less danger of injury from putting the spade and the hoe into the hands of a large proportion of insane persons, than from shutting them up together in idleness, though under the guards of straps, straitwaistcoats, or chains. He subsequently introduced the system of labour into Hanwell ... as a means of promoting the cure and the comfort of the patients. Much has been said in favour of amusing occupations for the insane; and they are certainly not to be overlooked ... but they are not to be compared, as regards their beneficial influence on the mind, with those occupations in which a man labours to some useful end.

[1] Carl Wiegant Maximilian Jacobi (1775–1858), M.D. ERFURT, medical superintendent of the Asylum at Siegburg near Bonn. In 1822 he translated Tuke's *Description* in *Sammlungen fuer die Heilkunde der Gemuethskrankheiten*, Elberfeld. A few extracts had appeared earlier in Nasse's *Zeitschrift fuer psychische Aerzte*, 1820. In 1834 during his third visit to England Jacobi presented Tuke with a copy of his *Ueber die Anlegung und Einrichtung von Irren-Heilanstalten*, Berlin 1834. 'Being ignorant of the German language' wrote Tuke, 'I availed myself of the knowledge of my friend John Kitching, then a medical pupil at the Retreat [for eleven years apprentice and assistant to the superintendent; M.R.C.S., L.S.A. 1839; later superintendent in succession to Thurnam 1849–74) to become acquainted with many passages of the work: these specimens led me to obtain a translation of the whole, with the view of presenting it to the English reader'. Tuke's introduction of 72 pages was in turn translated into German by Dr. N. H. Julius in *Beitraege zur britischen Irrenheilkunde*, Berlin 1844.

As late as 1850 when Tuke was already in poor health, he drew up a memorandum containing suggestions for improvements at the Retreat in which he stressed the need in this way to relieve the monotony which he was sure retarded the recovery of patients and dispirited the officers:

> Ever since I became connected with the Retreat ... I have been strongly impressed with the conviction, that the monotony which prevails within its walls is one of the greatest impediments to its curative treatment ... What we want ... is the engagement of the mind in the pursuit of some rational object, in which it can feel an interest ... Even a superficial observation of the aspect and conduct of the insane ... will convince us that they are, to a very large extent, subject to the same influences as the sane. Such considerations have been the foundation of moral treatment at the Retreat from its rise to the present time ... It has long struck me that in many cases we might advantageously keep up more than we do, the genuine idea of our establishment, – that of a *hospital* for the treatment of mental affections.

PARIS–EDINBURGH–THOMAS HODGKIN–JOHN CONOLLY

Samuel Tuke visited almost every asylum in England, Scotland and Ireland, and a number on the Continent. In 1824 he went to Paris with an introduction to Esquirol whose assistant Mitivié showed him round the Salpêtrière and his private establishment. He also saw the Bicêtre accompanied by Dr. Pariset and concluded that although the French 'might certainly take some useful lessons from us ... there is also a good deal to be learned from them'.

In April 1821 he went to the general meeting of Friends at Edinburgh. There 'I found ... Thomas Hodgkin[1] studying medicine, and he became my constant companion during my stay. We visited the Bridewell, the prison, the asylum [Edinburgh Royal Asylum at Morningside, opened 1813], and the libraries ... I left with T. Hodgkin and Thomas Fisher, another Friend student, for Lanark' – to see the great social experiment of Robert Owen. Tuke's influence on the young students must have been considerable since Hodgkin retained his interest in insanity and was in fact one of the expert witnesses called at the trial of Edward Oxford in 1840 for shooting at Queen Victoria (where Conolly also gave evidence); and Fisher took insanity as the subject of his M.D. thesis *Dissertatio medica inauguralis de insania*, Edinburgh 1822, dedicated to 'Samueli Tuke ... viro benevolo ac ornato'. After graduation Hodgkin looked after the health of Tuke's family for many years.

But historically the most significant event – although undocumented – was Hodgkin's introduction of Conolly to Tuke. Conolly is known to have been a student friend of Hodgkin and was at that time preparing for his M.D. thesis *De statu mentis in insania et melancholia*, Edinburgh 1821, which he presented in August and which shows on almost every page

[1] Thomas Hodgkin (1798–1866), M.D. EDIN., L.R.C.P., physician and morbid anatomist known for his first description of what in his honour Sir Samuel Wilks named 'Hodgkin's disease', who never got on the staff of Guy's Hospital because he wore Quaker dress and was associated with the liberal London University and the Aborigines' Protection Society.

how enthusiastic he was about the Retreat. Some twenty years later Tuke recorded his visit to Conolly at Hanwell in his introduction to Jacobi's book: 'From the zeal, talents, and integrity of Dr. Conolly, we shall doubtless learn in the most satisfactory manner, the further results of this large and most satisfactory experiment' – the total abolition of mechanical restraint, the logical conclusion of the pioneer work of the Tukes. And in 1852 he wrote to his son 'I find the portrait of Dr. Conolly [the engraving by W. Walker of the painting by Sir John Watson Gordon of 1851] is ready for delivery. I ... wish thee to accept from me the proof copy which I am entitled to, and thou can have put it into a frame ... I presume thou wilt attend Dr. Conolly's lectures this summer' – and indeed Daniel Hack Tuke was one of the two students from St. Bartholomew's Hospital chosen in 1852 to attend Conolly's clinical demonstrations at Hanwell.

Conolly himself always freely acknowledged his indebtedness to Samuel Tuke. In his magnum opus *The treatment of the insane without mechanical restraints*, 1856 he wrote:

> For readers desirous to know the views which ought to prevail in all lunatic asylums, I could not even now refer to any work in which they are more perspicuously explained than in Samuel Tuke's account of the Retreat ... The substitution of sympathy for gross unkindness, severity, and 'stripes'; the diversion of the mind from its excitements and griefs by various occupations; and a wise confidence in the patients when they promised to control themselves, led to the prevalence of order and neatness and nearly banished furious mania from this wisely devised place of recovery.

And reminiscing in 1860 Conolly wrote again of the 'deep impression ... derived from the perusal, again and again, even when still a student, of that excellent "Description of the Retreat"... which I would still urge every student to read, and to add to his library'.

A NEW EDITION

Within three years of publication the *Description* was sold out. Indeed the previous year the publishers had appended a note to *Practical hints* that all octavo copies had been sold out but that a few 'in 4to, fine paper, extra boards, 12s.' remained. On 16 February 1817 just before Dr. Spurzheim visited the Retreat, Tuke wrote in his diary: 'Commenced tonight the preparation of a new edition of the "Description" '. Unfortunately it never appeared, although he continued with its preparation for some time, since in April 1820 he sent to Dr. George Mann Burrows the statistics of the Retreat from its opening to the end of 1819 which he had assembled for it. Burrows incidentally admired the moral treatment of the Retreat but 'viewed with regret the little confidence professed by the benevolent conductors ... in ... the great efficacy of medicine in the majority of cases of insanity'. Twenty years later Thurnam included in his book on the statistics of insanity a historical sketch of the Retreat compiled from Tuke 'in some degree, to supply the place formerly occupied by the "Description" ... which has been long out of print; but which ... formed so important a contribution ... and ... marks the epoch of the spread of more enlightened views as to the treatment of insanity'.

Samuel himself did not refer to a second edition again until 1852, when his son, then still a medical student, revived the idea and proposed making the necessary revision himself. 'What would be thy plan for a new edition' wrote father to son, 'should it not be a continued history of the improvements in the treatment of the insane', adding with characteristic humbleness 'And would not the additions be more than the original work?' Even then a second edition did not materialise, but the son's classic *Chapters in the history of the insane in the British Isles*, 1882 may be so regarded since it presented the spirit and the achievements of the Retreat as the watershed dividing the old psychiatry from the new, and showed how the great asylum era of the 19th century owed to it its impetus.

In the same year 1852, as if his own early ambitions to become a doctor and specialise in insanity had been revived, Samuel wrote to his son:

> I was this morning thinking of thee as having entered on thy professional course, and persisting in thy early, and I think later views, as to making the treatment of mental diseases thy primary object. It passed my mind that, perhaps, after having gained some further experience, thou might advantageously give or publish – possibly both – a few popular lectures 'on mental diseases, the means of their prevention and of their treatment in the more incipient stages'. I thought something of the programme of the lectures ...

DECLINING YEARS

From 1848 Samuel Tuke's health declined and he suffered repeated strokes. In 1849 he retired from the committees of the York Asylum and the Retreat, but retained the post of treasurer until 1853. In the summer of 1855 Dorothea Lynde Dix stayed a few weeks with him. 'The American invader' as she was affectionately called, who did so much to provide hospitals for the mentally ill in America and whose visit to the British Isles resulted in many improvements incorporated chiefly in the *Act for the Regulation of the Care and Treatment of Lunatics ... in Scotland*, 1857, must have wakened many memories. For more than half a century he had had 'a great interest in the welfare of the insane' as he wrote to Miss Dix's compatriot Dr. John S. Butler of the Hartford Retreat. 'Their miserable condition ... when I set out in life, deeply affected me, and bound me to unite with the few who were then labouring to improve it, and I do rejoice that so much has ... been effected ... It is therefore particularly grateful to me, that our Anglo-American brethren are exerting themselves so much ... to improve the condition of the insane in their young country'.

Two years later on 14 October 1857 at the age of 74 'Mr. Tuke of York ... known all over the world as one of the most enlightened friends of the insane' died. His only public honour came in November 1841 when the newly founded Association of Medical Officers of Asylums and Hospitals for the Insane, now the Royal Medico-Psychological Association, at its first annual general meeting held at Nottingham Asylum, elected him its first honorary member.

NOTES TO TUKE'S *DESCRIPTION*

Page

v 'Recent subject of legislation' refers to the *Act for the better care and maintenance of lunatics, being paupers or criminals in England*, 1808 (48 Geo. III, c. 96), known as Wynn's Act.

ix John Haslam (1764–1844), apothecary to Bethlem Hospital 1795–1816.
Philippe Pinel (1745–1826), at that time physician to the Salpêtrière, the great French physician and psychiatrist and reformer of the treatment of the insane.

x George Jepson (1745–1836) was in charge of the day to day running of the Retreat from 1797–1822. A self-taught man, originally a weaver, he had acquired a knowledge of medicine and a measure of local fame as counsellor and practitioner in a rural district in the West Riding. In 1806 he married Katherine Allen (1776–1844) who had come to the Retreat in charge of the female department in 1796 from Dr. Edward Long Fox's Asylum at Cleve Hill, near Bristol. For twenty-five years they were responsible for the practical conduct of the Retreat and retired together.

xi William Belcombe, M.D. Goettingen, third visiting physician to the Retreat 1802–26, was joined by Samuel Tuke's brother-in-law Caleb Williams, Surgeon, in 1824 and succeeded by his son Henry Stephens Belcombe, M.D. Edin., friend of Charles Dickens.

Dr. Thomas Fowler (?–1801), M.D. Edin., first visiting physician to the Retreat from 1796 until his death. He started his career as an apothecary or general practitioner at York, then became physician at the Stafford Infirmary, and finally returned to York. He wrote a number of books of which the best known are *Medical reports, of the effects of tobacco, principally with regard to its diuretic quality*, 1785; and *Medical reports of the effect of arsenic, in the cure of agues, remitting fevers, and periodic headachs … Together with a letter from Dr. [Thomas] Arnold, of Leicester, and another from Dr. [William] Withering, describing their experience*, 1786, in which he introduced the medicinal use of inorganic arsenic or 'Fowler's solution', which is still in use.

22 The girl's name was Hannah Mills and she takes her place beside William Norris at Bethlem Hospital as one of the two martyrs whose deaths changed the course of English psychiatric history. The records of the Friends Meeting House at York show that she actually died 30 April 1790, not 1791; the order for her burial was signed by Henry Tuke.

24 Lindley Murray (1745–1826), came of a leading New York Quaker merchant family. After a successful career at the bar he retired in 1784

to England and settled at Holgate near York. There he became famous for his botanical garden, his library, his philanthropy, and above all for his *English grammar*, 1795, written for the girls' school founded by William and Esther Tuke which Samuel attended.

41 The architect of the Retreat was John Bevans of London, perhaps the father of James Bevans, architect of Grays-Inn, whose plans for a London Asylum, visualised by Edward Wakefield and his friends to provide optimum conditions for the new mild care and moral treatment pioneered at the Retreat, were presented to the Parliamentary Committee of 1815 and are reproduced in its *Report*. Unfortunately it never materialised.

44 William Tuke visited various establishments during these years to obtain information, including St. Luke's in London 'but was afresh impressed with the necessity of some such institution as the Retreat, by what he witnessed there', in particular seeing 'the patients miserably coerced'.

46 Timothy Maud (?–1796) retired practitioner of Bradford and William Tuke's brother-in-law, first superintendent of the Retreat, died two months after taking office. He was chosen because the office required 'a solid Friend with some medical knowledge … capable of superintending the institution under the direction of a Physician'.

61 Robert Cappe (?–1802), M.D. Edin., second physician to the Retreat. His stepmother Catherine Cappe took a special interest in the insane and was one of Benjamin Rush's favourite correspondents. She became 'lady visitor' of the York Asylum appointed after the troubles of 1813–4, and probably also of the Retreat where 'lady visitors' had been appointed from its opening. She was the authoress of *On the desireableness and utility of ladies visiting the female wards of hospitals and lunatic asylums*, York 1817.

94 Gaspar Charles de la Rive, M.D. Edin., L.R.C.P., a political refugee from Switzerland who later returned to Geneva where he practised. He sent from England a glowing report of his visit to the Retreat, which was published in *Bibliothèque Britannique*, 1798, part of which Tuke appended in translation.

106 William Stark (?–1813), architect of the Glasgow Royal Lunatic Asylum at Gartnavel which opened 1814, author of *Remarks on the construction of public hospitals for the cure of mental derangement*, Edinburgh 1807 (a second edition with additional matter Glasgow 1810). It was the first work on the construction of mental hospi-

Page

106 tals by a professional architect. While planning the Glasgow Asylum he visited the Retreat of which he wrote 'It is a government of humanity and of consummate skill, and requires no aid from the arm of violence, or the exertions of brutal force ... A great deal of delicacy appears in the attentions paid to the smaller feelings of the patients .. when I visited them, the managers were occupied in contriving how to get rid of the bolts with which the patients are shut up at night, on account of their harsh ungrateful sound, and of their communicating to the asylum somewhat of the air and character of a prison ... however desirable a good system of management may be, no such system can be prosecuted with effect in an ill contrived building'.

Robert Reid (1776–1856), last holder of the office of King's architect in Scotland, designer of the Royal Edinburgh Asylum at Morningside which opened in 1813, and author of 'Observations on the structure of hospitals for the treatment of lunatics', an article in *Observations on the structure of hospitals for the treatment of lunatics*, Edinburgh 1809, edited by Andrew Dun-

Page

can sen.

113 Robert Darling Willis (1760–1821), M.D.Edin., F.R.C.P.,son of the Reverend Dr. Francis Willis, the well-known clerical mad-doctor, attended George III with his father in 1788–9, and again in 1810. In 1807 as College of Physicians Commissioner under the *Act for regulating madhouses*, 1774, he gave evidence before the *Select Committee appointed to enquire into the state of lunatics*, from the report of which Tuke quotes.

137 For earlier observations on the effect of fever on insanity see John Monro's *Remarks on Dr. Battie's treatise on madness*, 1758 (reprinted in Psychiatric Monograph Series No. 3, 1962).

142 William Cowper was well qualified to write about the effects of restraint on the mind since he was a patient for two years 1763–5 in Dr. Nathaniel Cotton's madhouse at St. Albans.

172 Fixing or 'setting' the patient by the eye was a means of gaining moral ascendency over him described by William Pargeter in *Observations on maniacal disorders*, Reading 1792 and popularised by the Reverend Dr. Francis Willis.

DESCRIPTION

OF

THE RETREAT,

AN INSTITUTION NEAR YORK

𝕱𝖔𝖗 𝕴𝖓𝖘𝖆𝖓𝖊 𝕻𝖊𝖗𝖘𝖔𝖓𝖘

OF THE

SOCIETY OF FRIENDS.

CONTAINING AN ACCOUNT OF ITS

ORIGIN AND PROGRESS,

𝕿𝖍𝖊 𝕸𝖔𝖉𝖊𝖘 𝖔𝖋 𝕿𝖗𝖊𝖆𝖙𝖒𝖊𝖓𝖙,

AND

A STATEMENT OF CASES,

—◆—

By SAMUEL TUKE.

—◆—

With an Elevation and Plans of the Building.

YORK:

PRINTED FOR W. ALEXANDER, AND SOLD BY HIM;
SOLD ALSO BY M. M. AND E. WEBB, BRISTOL:
AND BY DARTON, HARVEY, AND CO.; WILLIAM PHILLIPS; AND
W. DARTON, LONDON.

1813.

(Thomas Wilson and Sons, Printers, High-Ousegate, York)

TO

WILLIAM TUKE,

THE FIRST ACTIVE PROMOTER

OF THE ESTABLISHMENT

DESCRIBED IN THE FOLLOWING PAGES,

AND

TO WHOSE PERSEVERING EXERTIONS

FOR ITS WELFARE,

UNRELAXED AT THE ADVANCED AGE OF EIGHTY YEARS,

MUCH OF ITS PRESENT REPUTATION

MAY JUSTLY BE ATTRIBUTED;

THIS WORK IS

(WITHOUT HIS KNOWLEDGE)

MOST RESPECTFULLY INSCRIBED,

BY HIS AFFECTIONATE GRANDSON,

SAMUEL TUKE.

Engd by R. Scotchfield Editor.

PERSPECTIVE VIEW of the NORTH FRONT of the RETREAT near YORK.

PREFACE.

———◆———

At the present time, when a considerable degree of interest is excited respecting the treatment of insane persons, and when the government of our country has recently made it a subject of legislation, it is presumed that any account of existing Institutions, which may throw light on the method of treating this deplorable class of our fellow-creatures, will not be unacceptable to the public.

The Establishment which is described in the following pages, though on a small scale, has so far met the approbation of many judicious persons, who have had an opportunity of minutely inspecting its internal economy and management, that I have been induced to attempt such a representation, as it is hoped will

B

be useful to those who are engaged in similar Institutions.

Contemplating the loss of reason as pre-eminent in the catalogue of human afflictions; and believing that the experience of the Retreat throws some light on the means of its mitigation, and also that it has demonstrated, beyond all contradiction, the superior efficacy, both in respect of cure and security, of a mild system of treatment in all cases of mental disorder, an account of that experience has long appeared to me, due to the public.

They are not words of course when I say, I sincerely wish that the present work had been undertaken by some one more competent to do it justice, from professional knowledge, greater leisure, or superior ability. It seemed, however, to my mind, that the present was an important time for a publication of this nature, from the number of establishments which have been very recently formed, or which are now in contemplation. I therefore conceived that the

injury of delay would probably exceed the disadvantages arising from the many imperfections
which I was well aware would attend my performance. If it should be thought to afford
satisfactory evidence in favour of a more mild
system of treatment, than has been generally
adopted ; if it should also prove, which I flatter
myself it will, the practicability of introducing
such a system into establishments for the insane
poor, whose situation has in general been too
pitiable for words to describe, I shall esteem
myself peculiarly happy in this publication.
I shall then, having no pretensions to literary
merit, confidently bespeak the candour of the
reader, to the faults of imperfect arrangement
or inelegant expression.

It is probable that some readers will think,
that a more minute account is given of the
practices of the Retreat than was necessary ;
but inquiries, which have recently been made
by intelligent persons interested in similar
undertakings, may be alleged in justifica-
tion.

Apology, however, is due to the general reader for the length of the two first chapters, which have much exceeded the original design. This has been occasioned by the wishes of many subscribers to the Institution, who could not obtain a regular series of reports, to have a particular detail of its origin and progress.

It is much to be regretted, that we possess so few accounts of the mode of treatment, and the success of establishments, for the relief of insanity. The want of facts relative to this subject, and our disposition to hasty generalization, have led to many conclusions, equally unfriendly to the progress of knowledge, and the comfort of the patients.

The interests of humanity and science, alike call upon us to communicate freely the discoveries we make, or the failures which happen to us, in a pursuit so intimately connected with the happiness of our species. If persons engaged in the management of the insane,

were more generally to publish the result of
their observations, we might reasonably hope
that the causes of this obscure and affecting
disorder would receive some illustration. We
might at least confidently expect to ascertain,
with greater precision, its general laws; and,
from a comparison of the modes and success of
various establishments, should be able to infer
the most probable means of rescuing, or
relieving the unhappy victims of this disease.

It has been remarked, that " Physicians,
attending generally to diseases, have not
been reserved, in imparting to the public the
amount of their labours and success : but, with
regard to this disorder, those who have devoted
their whole attention to its treatment, have
either been negligent, or cautious of giving
information respecting it."* Surely, as the
intelligent Pinel observes, after a similar complaint, " He who cultivates the science of medicine, as a branch of natural history, pursues a

---

* Haslam's Observations, p. 244.

more frank and open system of conduct, nor
seeks to conceal the obstacles which he meets
with in his course. What he discovers, he feels
no reluctance to show; and the difficulties which
he cannot master, he leaves, with the impression
of his hand upon them, for the benefit of his
successors in the same route." *

In justice to the work, as well as to individuals, it is proper to state, that if the public are
at all benefited by the information contained
in the present publication, they are chiefly indebted to my worthy friend GEORGE JEPSON,
the superintendent and apothecary of the
Retreat. Having filled these offices nearly
from its commencement, and having, by
his talents and humanity, carried into effect
the benevolent wishes of the original promoters
of this Establishment, beyond their most sanguine expectations, he was the only person
who could furnish me with the documents
which my plan rendered necessary: and had

---

* Treatise on Insanity, translated by Dr. Davis.

I not been assured of his cordial assistance, the work would not have been attempted. The arduous nature of the duties which he so usefully fulfils, will furnish sufficient apology for his not having performed it, instead of furnishing the materials; and it affords me some satisfaction to reflect, that contemplating the uncertainty of human life, a part at least of his knowledge is now communicated.

I am also indebted to my friend Dr. BEL-COMBE, the present skilful physician to the Institution, for several valuable hints on the perusal of the manuscript; and to the widow of the late Dr. FOWLER, for the readiness with which she communicated to me several very useful notes and papers which he had made or collected, during his attendance at the Retreat.

I hope that my partiality for the establishment which I have endeavoured to describe, and my wish to present its objects and regulations to the public eye, have not induced me to deviate from that candour and sobriety of representation, which the reader has a right to expect. I am not conscious of such a deviation : but I well know that strong attachments, unless carefully guarded, are apt to impose upon our judgment. That this, however, has not been the case, in the present instance, I am encouraged to believe, from the very favourable and commendatory characters which have been given of the Institution, by several well-informed and impartial persons, by whom it has been visited, and minutely examined. *

---

* It may be proper to observe, that, though the patients are never exhibited to gratify the curiosity of visiters, yet professional persons, or those peculiarly interested in the subject, are permitted at all seasonable hours, to visit *every part* of the establishment. It would be well if this plan were generally adopted in other Institutions of this nature, as the uncertainty of visiters arriving would be some check upon neglect, or improper conduct.

It may also be proper to state, that several persons about to engage in the superintendence of similar establishments, have made a temporary residence in York, and have been permitted by the Committee of the Retreat to observe daily the economy of the house, and the mode of managing the patients.

To support the statements given in this work of the modes of treatment at the Retreat, a few respectable testimonies in its favour are given in an Appendix. I am, however, far from imagining that this Asylum is a perfect model for others, either in regard to construction or management. If several improvements have been successfully introduced, it is probable that many others remain unattempted. The managers will not, I trust, allow the approbation they have already received, to induce a relaxation of their future endeavours to combine, in a still greater degree, the comfort with the security of the insane; but, on the contrary, that they will be stimulated by it to further exertions, and proceed, in some degree, upon the maxim, *that nothing has been done, whilst any thing remains to be done.*

TABLE OF CONTENTS.

CHAPTER I.—HISTORICAL ACCOUNT.

CHAPTER II.—HISTORICAL ACCOUNT.

CHAPTER III.—DESCRIPTION AND APPROPRIATION
OF THE GROUNDS AND HOUSE.

CHAPTER IV.—MEDICAL TREATMENT.

CHAPTER V.— MORAL TREATMENT.

SECTION I.—INTRODUCTORY OBSERVATIONS.

DESCRIPTION

OF

THE RETREAT, &c.

———◆———

CHAPTER I.

HISTORICAL ACCOUNT.

Origin——Difficulties——First Meeting of Friends on the subject in 1792——Resolutions——Subscriptions——Meetings of Subscribers——Amount of Subscriptions, and general Opinion of Friends respecting the Institution——Resolutions of a Meeting in 1793——Determination to build——Land purchased and Building commenced in 1794——Amount of Subscriptions——Necessary to borrow Money—— Rules agreed upon in 1795——Additional Subscriptions at this time——House very nearly completed——Committee appointed to engage Servants, and to admit Patients——West Wing ordered to be built First Month, 1796.

THE history of the rise and progress of establishments, which have been peculiarly serviceable to society, like the biography of eminent men, is both interesting and useful. The inquisitive and speculative mind, loves to trace the causes of every stri-

C

king object; and the practical philanthropist may derive considerable advantage, from an account of benevolent experiments that have been made by others.

The origin of the Institution which forms the subject of the following pages, has much the appearance of accident. In the year 1791, a female, of the Society of Friends, was placed at an establishment for insane persons, in the vicinity of the City of York; and her family, residing at a considerable distance, requested some of their acquaintance in the City to visit her. The visits of these Friends were refused, on the ground of the patient not being in a suitable state to be seen by strangers: and, in a few weeks after her admission, death put a period to her sufferings.

The circumstance was affecting, and naturally excited reflections on the situation of insane persons, and on the probable improvements which might be adopted in establishments of this nature. In particular, it was conceived that peculiar advantage would be derived to the Society of Friends, by having an Institution of this kind under their own care, in which a milder and more appropriate system of treatment, than that usually practised, might be adopted; and where, during lucid intervals, or the state of convalescence, the patient might enjoy the society of those who were of similar habits and opinions. It was thought, very justly, that the indiscriminate mixture, which must occur in large public establishments, of persons of opposite religious sentiments and practices ; of the profligate and the virtuous; the profane and the serious; was calculated to check the progress of re-turning reason, and to fix, still deeper, the melancholy and misanthropic train of ideas, which, in some descriptions of insanity, impresses the mind. It was believed also, that the general treatment of insane persons was, too frequently, calculated to depress and degrade, rather than to awaken the slumbering reason, or correct its wild hallucina-tions.

In one of the conversations to which the circum-stance before-mentioned gave rise, the propriety of attempting to form an Establishment for persons of our own Society, was suggested to William Tuke, whose feelings were already much interested in the subject, and whose persevering mind, rendered him peculiarly eligible to promote such an undertaking. After mature reflection, and several consultations with his most intimate friends* on the subject, he was decidedly of opinion, that an Establishment for the insane of our own Society, of every class in regard to property, was both eligible and highly desirable. It was necessary to excite a general interest in the Society on the subject. He therefore, after the close of the Quarterly Meeting at York, in the 3d Month, 1792, requested Friends to allow him to introduce to them a subject, connected with the welfare of the Society. He then stated the views which he, and those whom he had consulted, had taken of this subject; the circumstance which had given rise to their interest respecting it, and the conviction which had resulted in their minds, in favour of an Institution under the government of Friends, for the care and accommodation of their own Members, labouring under that most afflictive dispensation—the loss of reason.

Few objections were then made, and several persons appeared to be impressed with the importance of the subject, and the propriety of the proposed measure.

---

* Amongst the most early and strenuous friends of this Establishment, I wish to particularize the name of the excellent Lindley Murray; to whose steady endeavours, for promoting its welfare, the Institution is much indebted.

The Friends with whom the proposal originated, were requested to prepare the outline of a plan, for the consideration of those who might attend the next Quarterly Meeting. Several objections, however, on a variety of grounds, soon afterward appeared. Many Friends were acquainted with but few, if any, objects for such an Establishment; and they seemed to forget that there might probably be many cases with which they were not acquainted. Some were not sensible that any improvement could be made in the treatment of the insane; supposing that the privations, and severe treatment, to which they were generally exposed, were necessary in their unhappy situation; and others, seemed rather averse to the concentration of the instances of this disease amongst us.

It was not, however, at all surprising that considerable diversity of opinion, should prevail upon a subject which was entirely new, and foreign to the general inquiries of those to whom it was proposed; and we must not forget that there was a respectable number, who duly appreciated the advantages likely to accrue to the Society from the proposed Establishment, and who cordially engaged in the promotion of the design. To these persons, and to the steady exertions of its chief promoter, whose mind

was not to be deterred by ordinary difficulties, the
Society of Friends, may justly be said to owe the advan·
tages it derives from this admirable Institution.

Proposals for raising money and forming the
Establishment, were prepared and laid before Friends,
at the conclusion of the next Quarterly Meeting ;
which were generally approved.   A subscription was
immediately entered into; and the contributions were
one hundred pounds, for a life-annuity of five per cent.
per annum ; annual subscriptions £11 : 0 : 6 for three
years certain, and donations amounting to £192 : 3s.
The following minutes were also made at this Meet‑
ing, viz.

" *At a Meeting of Friends held at York the 28th of*
6th Month, 1792, for the purpose of taking into
consideration the propriety of providing a retired
Habitation, with necessary advice, attendance, &c.
for the Members of our Society, and others in pro‑
fession with us, who may be in a state of Lunacy,
or so deranged in mind (not Idiots) *as to require*
such a provision ;

RESOLVED,

" *That persons of this description, (who are truly objects*
of great sympathy and compassion,) are often, from
the peculiar treatment which they require, necessarily

committed, wholly, to the government of people of
other Societies; by which means the state of their own
minds, and the feelings of their near connexions,
are rendered more dissatisfied and uncomfort-
able than would probably be the case, if they were
under the notice and care of those, with whom they
are connected in Religious Society. It appears,
therefore, very desirable that an Institution should
be formed, wholly under the government of Friends,
for the relief and accommodation of such Persons
of all ranks, with respect to property. This would
doubtless, in some degree, alleviate the anxiety of
the relatives, render the minds of the Patients more
easy in their lucid intervals, and consequently tend
to facilitate and promote their recovery——

IT IS THEREFORE PROPOSED,

1st. "THAT, in case proper encouragement be given,
Ground be purchased, and a Building be erected, sufficient to accommodate Thirty Patients, in an airy
situation, and at as short a distance from York as may
be, so as to have the privilege of retirement; and that
there be a few acres for keeping cows, and for garden
ground for the family; which will afford scope for
the Patients to take exercise, when that may be pru-
dent and suitable.

C 4

2d. " THAT the Institution be established and supported by annuities, donations, and annual subscriptions; and that the same (which should be altogether
voluntary) be promoted amongst Friends, within
the compass of this, and any other Quarterly Meeting.

3d. " THAT each Subscriber, by way of annuity,
contributing a sum not less than Twenty Pounds,
shall receive an interest of five per cent. per ann.
during life; and as the undertaking may not be able
to pay this interest, and otherwise maintain itself for
the first three years, those entered as Subscribers for
annual payments, be engaged for three years certain,
in case the Subscriber should so long live.

4th. " THAT a contribution of One Hundred Pounds,
from any Quarterly Meeting in its collective capacity,
paid to the Treasurer of this Institution before the year
1794; or a donation, at any time, of Twenty-five
Pounds from any Friend; or a subscription of Fifty
Pounds for an annuity, shall entitle such Quarterly
Meeting, Donor, or Annuitant, respectively, to the
privilege of nominating one *poor* patient at a time
on the lowest terms of admission.

5th. " THAT the name of every annuitant, donor, and subscriber, be recorded in a book to be kept for that purpose ; and that every Annuitant, Donor of not less than Two Guineas, and Subscriber of sums in any manner equal to Two Guineas, in the first three years, (being and continuing a member of our Society,) shall be a Member of the Meetings which are to be held for the government and superintendence of the Institution.

6th. " THAT there be paid for board, washing, medical advice, medicines, and all other things necessary except clothing, according to the circumstances of the Patients or their friends, from four shillings to fifteen shillings per week, or higher in particular cases ; and six shillings per week for the board of the Servant of a Patient, in case the friends of any patient should incline to send one; which servant must be approved by the Committee.

7th. " THAT eight shillings per week and upwards, according to circumstances, be the terms for patients who come from the compass of any other Quarterly Meeting than Yorkshire, unless privileged agreeably to the 4th proposal.—These terms for patients to be subject to future alteration, if found necessary.

" WILLIAM TUKE is desired to get one thousand copies of these proposals printed, and circulated amongst Friends; with an account of the Subscriptions which have been or may be made previously to the printing thereof."

A number of Friends, residing in different parts of the county of York, were appointed to solicit subscriptions from the members of their respective meetings, towards the proposed Establishment; and they were desired to bring an account of their success to the next Meeting, to be held three months from the time of the first. At the second Meeting, the additional subscriptions were few and trifling; consisting only of £50 to the Annuities, £24 : 3s. to the Donations, and £1 : 1s. to the Annual Subscriptions. Considerable additions were, however, brought to the third and fourth Meetings; and the active promoters of the Establishment, had the pleasure of witnessing an increase of interest in the minds of their friends in general, towards the subject.

Variety of opinion, as might naturally be expected, still prevailed, with regard to the necessity of the proposed measure; and there was considerable diversity of sentiment, amongst those who approved of the general design, as to the best manner of executing it. At the fourth Meeting it was therefore thought advisable, to republish the proposals of the first Meeting, with an answer to the principal objections which had been made to them, and with an account of the subscriptions at that period. This paper, as it marks the progress of the Institution, and the general opinion of Friends respecting it, is given at length, with the exception of the Rules first proposed, which have been already inserted.

"YORK, *5th of 4th Month*, 1793.

"*At a Meeting of Friends it was agreed, that* 1500 *copies more of the preceding Proposals, with the following additional Minutes, and further Explanations, should be printed and circulated amongst Friends.*

"27*th of* 9*th Month*, 1792.

" As the benefit of the proposed Institution is intended to be extended to those who are not strictly Members of our Society, it is the judgment of this Meeting, that subscriptions may also be received from such persons."

" 5*th of* 4*th Month*, 1793.

" It having been objected that, according to the expression of the 7th Proposal, there appears to be an extraordinary privilege intended to Friends in Yorkshire, this Meeting thinks proper to disclaim having had such an intention. The prospect in forming the same was, that as the Subscriptions were set on foot in this County, they would amount to, at least, as many hundred pounds as there would be poor patients belonging to this Quarterly Meeting, at any one time in the House. But, in order to remove all doubts on that head, it is agreed, that the Quarterly Meeting of York, shall not enjoy any privilege superior to other subscribing Counties ; it being intended, that all Subscribers, whether they consist of Quarterly, or other Meetings, or of Individuals, shall enjoy the privilege of recommending poor patients, in proportion to their subscriptions, notwithstanding any expressions in the 4th or 7th proposals, that may bear a different construction.

" In case any Quarterly Meeting be so small, or its members not in an eligible situation to raise One Hundred Pounds, the General Meeting of Subscribers shall have a power, on application, to extend the privilege of the 4th proposal to such Meetings, on contributing a smaller sum, at the discretion of the said General Meeting.

"It is agreed that when the Annuities and Donations amount to One Thousand Pounds, the application thereof shall be taken under consideration, by a General Meeting of Subscribers."

THE FOLLOWING IS THE PRESENT STATE OF SUBSCRIPTIONS.

For Annuities.

	£.	s.	d.
Yorkshire, one Subscriber, ...	100	0	0
Ditto, ... one	50	0	0
Suffolk, .. two of £.50 each, ...	100	0	0
Yorkshire, one	25	0	0
	£275	0	0

Annual for Three Years.

	£.	s.	d.
Yorkshire, three of 2gs.	6	6	0
Ditto, ... sixteen of 1 guinea, ...	16	16	0
Ditto, ... one of half a guinea, ...	0	10	6
	£ 23	12	6

Donations.

	£.	s.	d.
Yorkshire, one, ...	52	10	0
London, .. one, ...	21	0	0
Suffolk, several of £25 each, to one guinea, ..	118	1	0
Yorkshire, nine of 10gs.	94	10	0
London, .. one .. ditto, ...	10	10	0
Yorkshire, one	8	8	0
Ditto, ... two ..... of 6gs.	12	12	0
Ditto, ... twenty-nine of 5gs.	152	5	0
Ditto, ... five ..... of 3gs.	15	15	0
Ditto, ... ten ...... of 2gs.	21	0	0
Ditto, ... one	1	11	6
Ditto, ... seven .... of 1 guinea, ...	7	7	0
Ditto, ... two ..... of half a guinea, ..	1	1	0
	£516	10	6

" As several objections have been made, especially by
Friends at a distance, to some parts of the fore-
going Plan, the following remarks and explana-
tions are added, in order to remove them.

" Some have thought that accommodations for so
many as thirty patients, should not have been aimed
at: But it is obvious, that the quantity of ground for
exercise, ought not to be much, if any, less for fifteen
than for thirty; that kitchens, parlours, and almost
all parts of the building, except the number of patients' rooms, ought to be nearly the same; and that
it would make little difference with respect to Physician and domestic Managers : So that to accommodate the proposed number, would not only lessen the
expense of each patient, but extend the benefits of
the Institution to Friends at a greater distance.

" The situation of York, and its distance from some
parts, both in the North and South, have been stated
as principal objections. With respect to the place,
it was thought best to fix it at the beginning, as the
consideration of so material a point afterwards, might
have afforded a subject of much altercation; and the
different views of Subscribers, might then produce diversity of sentiments, to the great embarrassment of
the undertaking. It should be attended to, that the

proposal originated in Yorkshire; and that, though the views of Friends there, were not confined to that county, they did not consider the Institution as likely to accommodate the Society in the whole nation; and therefore, whilst they judged York to be an eligible situation for a limited undertaking of this nature, thay have been desirous that its privileges should be extended to Friends in general, upon reasonable conditions; as Patients, even in low circumstances, are often sent very far; one, in particular, having been lately taken 120 miles to Manchester; and divers have been sent from Yorkshire to London.

" It appears necessary, that General Meetings of the Subscribers should be held once a Year, to receive Reports of the preceding year's accounts, make Rules, and appoint Committees, &c. To collect subscribers for these purposes might be difficult, unless they were drawn together on some particular occasion: The Quarterly Meeting of York affords such an occasion better than any other, because it is larger, and Friends more frequently come to it from distant parts. Besides, if a Committee should meet Quarterly, it may then be conveniently appointed of Friends, residing in various and distant parts of the

County. This Committee may appoint Visitors, and a Sub-committee of Friends conveniently situated, to take the immediate oversight of the Institution, and to make report to them once a Quarter.

" The price of land suitable for the purpose is much lower near York, than it is equally near most other populous places; and at such only, a good choice of medical assistance can be expected. The air also is healthy, and much more free from smoke than situations near manufacturing towns; and the country being generally fruitful and not populous, provisions are considerably cheaper than at such places. It may be further observed, that at a general Conference since the proposals were circulated, it was considered whether York was the most proper place; when there appeared a general acquiescence, and not a dissenting voice.

" With respect to the objections to the 4th proposal, it may be proper to remark, that a Quarterly Meeting being a standing body, its privilege is perpetual; but the right of a single Friend dies with him; and therefore, a Donation of £100 is required from the former, in its collective capacity, when only £25 Donation, or £50 Subscription for an Annuity, is required, to entitle a Friend to a similar privilege with a Quarterly Meeting. It should be attended to, that patients, whose connexions are of ability to pay eight shillings per week or upwards, according to circumstances, cannot be privileged under the 4th proposal. As to the other part of the objection to that proposal, it is apprehended that the minute now made will entirely remove it.

" It hath been said, that there are already many public Institutions of the kind, which render this unnecessary. But it is evident, besides what has been remarked on this head, in the former publication, that several peculiar and important advantages, will accrue from an Institution confined to ourselves. For as the disorder is a mental one, and people of regular conduct, and even religiously disposed minds, are not exempt from it, their confinement amongst persons in all respects strangers, and their promiscuous exposure to such company as is mostly found in public Institutions of this kind, must be peculiarly disgusting, and consequently augment their disorder. Nor is this idea merely chimerical; for it is well known, that the situation of divers Members of our Society, hath, from this cause, been unspeakably distressing. A circumstance which, it needs no arguments to

D

prove, must greatly retard, if not totally prevent their cure.

" It has hitherto been judged best not to trouble any Meeting of discipline with the establishment, or future management, of such an Institution, because matters of this sort are often worse than unedifying to these Meetings. So large a number of subscribers as there is likely to be, in the compass of York Quarterly Meeting, with others from distant parts who may attend, are likely to be fully competent to direct the management for many years to come ; and, before they are materially reduced in number, it will undoubtedly become their concern to provide for a regular succession.   But though it would not be proper, to introduce the whole management of the business in any Meeting for discipline ; yet the simple consideration of aiding the Establishment by subscriptions, may not be an improper subject for such a Meeting.   If one or more hundred pounds, should be raised and paid in its name, (the sums given by each Friend being specified or not, as they may choose,) such Meeting will not be subject to any future trouble, except that of keeping up an appointment of a friend or two, as agents, to correspond with the Committee, and recommend patients, &c.; similar to what has been done by divers Meetings, towards the support of hospitals in different parts of the nation.

" To conclude—an Institution of this nature must be fixed somewhere, and, unless it be on a very small scale, many patients must be sent from a considerable distance. Friends who think the object worthy their attention, may be encouraged to promote it, not only on a principle of charity to the poor, but even of compassion to those in easy and affluent circumstances; who will doubtless think themselves benefited, though they may pay amply for it. Those who have embarked in this undertaking, have not been influenced by interested views, nor are they requesting or desiring any favours for themselves. A malady, in many instances, the most deplorable that human nature is subject to, hath excited their sympathy and attention; and they invite such Friends as approve of their design, to co-operate with them in an Establishment, which hath for its object, the mitigation of misery, and the restoration of those, who are lost to civil and religious society: in the prosecution whereof, they humbly rely on the favour of HIM, whose tender mercies are over all his works."

D 2

Another Meeting of the friends to the Establishment, was held on the 27th of the 6th month, 1793, which adjourned to the time of the General Meeting at Ackworth School; where the sixth Meeting was held on the 31st of the 7th month. The Subscriptions offered for annuities amounted to £325; the donations to £799 : 13 : 6, and the annual subscriptions to £32 : 0 : 6. Inadequate as these funds were, even to purchase a sufficient quantity of land for the proposed Institution, in a suitable situation, the Meeting, deeply impressed with a sense of the importance and propriety of the proposed undertaking, confiding also in the generosity of their friends, when they should become more fully informed on the subject, nobly resolved to prosecute the Establishment in which they had so earnestly engaged. They accordingly appointed a number of Friends, to look out for a suitable situation and quantity of land, in the vicinity of York; and to make a purchase, if they thought proper. It was not, however, till the latter end of the year, that the Committee were able to make an eligible purchase. They then obtained the situation, which had first appeared to them in every respect desirable. Its distance was only half a mile from the walls of the city; the ground was elevated, and the situation afforded excellent air and water, as well as a very extensive and diversified prospect.

The quantity of land purchased, was nearly twenty acres; for which the sum of £2325 was agreed to be given. This being more than the Establishment was thought likely to require, about eight acres were immediately disposed of for the sum of £968, leaving above eleven acres at the cost of £1357.

An architect, and an eminent builder in London, were immediately consulted respecting the building; and their plans and estimates were laid before a Meeting in the 4th month, 1794. The estimate for the centre and the east wing, amounted to £1883 : 4 : 1; and, short as the funds still were of the expenses about to be incurred, the Meeting came to the determination, that the building should be speedily proceeded with; as it was hoped this would encourage Friends to come forward with additional subscriptions. Notwithstanding the endeavours which had been used to circulate information, relative to the proposed Establishment, it was apprehended that Friends, in many counties, were but little acquainted with the design; it was therefore agreed, at a

Meeting in the 9th month, 1794, to publish "fifteen hundred copies of the rules, with some small variations and explanations, and a list of subscriptions." These were directed to be circulated, as much as possible, within the compass of every Quarterly and Monthly Meeting in the nation.

The amount of subscriptions, of which an account was published at this time, was, for annuities £875; donations £1443 : 19 : 6; annual subscriptions engaged for three years £46 : 4s.

In the commencement of the following year, .1795, the building was covered in, and the inside work in great forwardness; but the funds being entirely expended, it was agreed, at a Meeting of Subscribers, "to borrow what might be necessary to complete the place for the reception of patients."

At a Meeting in the sixth month, a set of rules were proposed for the government of the Institution, copies of which were ordered to be printed, and given to each subscriber, that they might be fixed at the next Meeting. This was held in the ninth month, and the proposed rules, with but little alteration, were agreed upon ; but as modifications and additions have since been made, and the present rules will be found at the end of the 2d chapter of this work, it is unnecessary to detail here those which were then published.

The additions to the donations, at the close of this year, amounted only to £275 : 8s. ; and those to the annual subscriptions, to £5 : 5s. The building was now very nearly completed, and, at a Meeting on the 1st of 1st month, 1796, a Committee was appointed to engage proper persons to fill the various departments in the family. The next Meeting being informed, that the house was likely to be ready for the reception of a few patients, on or before the first of the sixth month following, appointed the same Friends to treat for the reception of patients, until another meeting. The Committee appointed to attend to the buildings, recommended that the shell of the west wing should be carried up ; and the Meeting directed that not only the shell, but the interior also should be completed.

Variety of sentiment, as might be expected, still continued to exist, as to the propriety of establishing a distinct receptacle for the insane of the Society of Friends. Only one opinion, however, could

D 4

reasonably be entertained, of the motives which actuated the strenuous supporters of such an Establishment; and they were gratified to observe, that the interest of their Friends respecting it, continued to increase, as the nature and object of their benevolent design, became more fully considered and developed.

Four years had now elapsed since the first Meeting, of the friends to the proposed Establishment; and they felt, as will naturally be supposed, a mixture of anxiety and pleasure, in contemplating the progress of their undertaking. But, confirmed, by further inquiry and observation, in the estimation of its importance; and relying on the favour of HIM, whose "mercies are over all his works," they looked forward with confidence to an increase of liberality, towards an Institution, which proposed to relieve the greatest of human afflictions.

CHAPTER II.

HISTORICAL ACCOUNT.

Opening of the House——Physician appointed——
Appointment and decease of the temporary Super-
intendent——Report of 1796——Present Conductors
engaged——Report 1797 and 1798——Additional
Building to the East Wing——Report 1799——
Rule respecting recent cases of Insanity——Report
1800, stating the benefit of early admission——
Report 1801——Decease of Dr. Fowler——Dr. Cappe
appointed his successor——Report 1802——Decease
of Dr. Cappe——Dr. Belcombe appointed Physi-
cian——Additional Building to the West Wing——
Reports 1803 to 1809——The Appendage proposed
and agreed to——Reports 1810 and 1811——Report
1812, stating the Appendage to be occupied, &c.——
General Remarks on the Institution——Summary of
Annual Reports on the Finances——Rules of the
Institution.

THE house being ready for the reception of
patients, according to the expectation given at the
last Meeting ; and a housekeeper and several
servants being provided, the house was opened on
the 11th of the 5th month, 1796, and three

patients were admitted, early in the following month. A Physician, resident in the city, was appointed to attend the house; but a suitable person for the important office of superintendent, was still wanted. The place, however, was temporarily supplied by the kindness of Timothy Maud, of Bradford, a Friend of great worth, as well as medical knowledge, who had retired from practice. The death of this benevolent person, in little more than two months, deprived the Establishment of his valuable services; and was at this time a serious loss to the Institution.

At the General Meeting of subscribers, on the 30th of 6th month, 1796, I find the following minute respecting the finances of the Institution, viz. 'The Committee reports, "That the additional wing of the building, as directed by the last Quarterly Meeting of subscribers, is in great forwardness; that the donations to this Institution amount to £1789 : 2 : 6; to which may be added fifty pounds fallen in by the decease of an annuitant; that the annual subscriptions amount to £51 : 9s.; that the Institution remains subject to the payment of five per cent. per annum, to life-annuitants, on the sum of £875; and that the several sums bor-

rowed on interest, towards completing the building,
amount to £1,245.' "

The difficulty of finding suitable persons to have
the superintendency of the family, occasioned the
Committee no small trouble and anxiety. In the
fifth month, however, of the following year, the
person who, at present, has the management of the
female department *, was happily engaged ; and
very shortly afterwards, the present superintendent
and apothecary entered on his arduous offices. The
conductors, and still more the unhappy objects of
this Establishment, have great reason to esteem as
a blessing, the appointment of these individuals.

The utility and excellence of all Institutions, however perfect in plan, must depend, in great measure,
upon the immediate managers; and what the poet
has said of political governments, applies with pecu-
lar force to establishments for the insane ;

" Whate'er is best administer'd, is best."

An inferior plan well executed, may be more beneficial than a better system, under neglected manage-

---

* The matron, or female superintendent, has the general care of the
patients, as well as of the domestic department.

ment. Perfection, however, can never be obtained,
without excellence in system, as well as in
practice.

The Report brought by the Committee to the
General Meeting, in the 6th month, 1797, states
that the total of subscriptions to this time, was,
for annuities £875; donations £2043 : 0 : 6; and
for annual subscriptions £46 : 4s.

The Committee in their Report, say: " In laying
before Friends the state of this Institution, we
apprehend it will be no small satisfaction to them
to be informed, that it is now agreeably supplied
with managers. The patients are under the care
of a Physician, who visits the house several times
a week; a man friend, well approved, hath undertaken the office of superintendent; and a woman
friend that of housekeeper; both of whom
have likewise a general oversight of the patients.
These, with two men and three women-servants
under them, form the present establishment of the
house.

" Though the great debt with which the Institution is encumbered, may lay those who have the

care of it under some difficulties, yet they conceive they are such as will not be insuperable, provided the Institution continue to possess the good opinion of the Society, with respect to its object, and that the management also prove satisfactory ; in which case it is hoped, that subscriptions and legacies will come in, so as not only to pay the interest of the debt, but also gradually to reduce the principal.

" Out of fifteen patients now in the house, seven are poor ones, on the low terms of 4s. per week ; the rest are from 8s. to £ 1 : 1s.—the income of the whole £ 6 : 5s. per week.

" From the experience already had, there is reason to believe, that when the number of patients in- crease, the Institution will be able to defray its own current expenses by the pay of the patients ; and though the terms are lower than those of any other Institution of the kind which we know of, yet, we presume, the accommodations are such as to render it suitable for those in any station of life* ; whether we regard the pleasantness and healthiness of the

---

* There are apartments in which patients, with a servant, may be accommodated, without mixing with the others."

situation, or the conveniences provided for the use
of the patients, both within doors and without; in
which we have studiously avoided that gloomy appearance, which frequently accompanies places appropriated for those, who are afflicted with disorders
of the mind.

" In the short time that this Institution has been
established, there has appeared abundant cause to
convince us of the necessity there was for it; for a
considerable disadvantage not only seems to have
been sustained, in many cases, from unskilful private
confinement; but there has also been particular occasion to observe the great loss, which individuals
of our Society have sustained, by being put under
the care of those, who are not only strangers to our
principles; but by whom they are frequently mixed
with other patients, who may indulge themselves
in ill language, and other exceptionable practices.
This often seems to leave an unprofitable effect
upon the patients' minds, after they are restored
to the use of their reason, alienating from those
religious attachments which they had before experienced; and, sometimes, even corrupting them
with vicious habits, to which they had been
strangers.

" In the infancy of such an Institution as this, they who have the principal management of it, do not conceive themselves superior to the disadvantages, which want of experience may be supposed to lay them under. They think, however, that they have abundant encouragement in the undertaking, not only from the great occasion there appears for such an Establishment, but also from the melioration of many of the patients. Since the opening of the house in 6th month 1796, to the same month 1797, eighteen patients have been admitted, most of whom, from the long continuance of their disorder, may be deemed incurables. Two patients have died, one is gone home recovered, and several others are greatly improved; and though symptoms of derangement in these may still be obvious, yet they appear, in general, more easy and comfortable, than, under such circumstances, might reasonably be expected.

" In describing the particular benefits of this undertaking, it seems proper to mention that of occasionally using the patients to such employment, as may be suitable and proper for them, in order to relieve the languor of idleness, and prevent the indulgence of gloomy sensations. The privilege of

attending religious meetings, when they are fit for
it, and of having occasionally the visits of suitable
Friends at the house, may be justly esteemed of no in-
considerable importance. These considerations, added
to those which have already been mentioned, and
that of the frequent attendance of women friends
appointed every month, by a Committee which
meets in the house, appear to give this Institution
peculiar advantages, in the view of Friends; and to
warrant the promoters of it in expecting the support
and encouragement of the Society."

The sum of £1300 was still wanted, to defray
the expenses attending the buildings; it was therefore agreed to endeavour to borrow that sum, at
the usual rate of interest.   The amount of £600
was immediately offered; and the remainder was
soon after obtained.

Several very liberal subscriptions were received
in the latter end of the year 1797, and in the commencement of 1798; so that the contributions
reported in the 6th month of this year, including
the annual subscriptions, amounted to £574 : 13 : 6;
and though the income from patients was only
£388 : 9 : 10, and the expenses amounted to

£ 697 : 7 : 7; yet the expenditure was exceeded by the total receipts, £ 268 : 5 : 9.

The managers of the Institution, could not but feel the most lively satisfaction, in thus witnessing, in great measure, the fulfilment of their hopes. In their annual Report of this year, they say: " In again laying before the subscribers, the state of this Institution, we feel encouragement from the liberal support which it has this year met with, from Friends in different parts of the nation ; as well as from repeated proofs of the advantages derived to the patients, by being under the care and government of persons, who are members of our Society. We think it, however, proper to observe, that out of twenty-three cases now in the house, all of them, except two or three, were, at their admission, of so long standing as to be considered incurable. Most of the patients appear much improved, and some of them may be considered in a state of recovery ; but from their liability to relapse, and their remote situation from home, their friends wait for further confirmation previously to their removal.

" Since the last Report, two patients have returned home recovered ; one of whom having relapsed,

E

has been re-admitted, which has also been the case with one returned last year. Nine others have been admitted this year; one of them, a few days after his admission, died of a fever. The number of patients now in the house, is nine men and fourteen women; eight of them are on the low terms of four shillings per week; the rest from eight shillings to one guinea.——The income from the whole is £9:15:0 per week. We are now in expectation that the income from the patients, will be nearly sufficient for their support and attendance; but the payment of annuities and interest, as well as the gradual reduction of the debt, will still require the pecuniary aid of those who approve of the Institution."

Several patients were admitted soon after the Report in 1798 was published; and it appeared nearly certain, that more accommodation than the present building. afforded, would very soon be requisite.

The Committee therefore proposed to the Quarterly Meeting of Directors, in the 9th month, the erection of an additional building, at the end of the east wing. There were at this time twenty-eight patients in the house; and as application had been received for the admission of several others, and the house was originally not adapted for more than thirty, the Meeting readily agreed to the proposal; and left the execution of it to the Committee.

A favourable account of the state of the Institution, was brought to the General Meeting in the 6th month, 1799; by which it appeared, that the income from patients this year, was very nearly sufficient for their support and attendance. The property of the Institution was increased this year £ 245; but the payment of life-annuities, and the interest of money borrowed, as well as the reduction of the principal, rendered the continued liberality of the friends of this establishment, highly desirable and necessary.

The directors observe, at this time, in their Report of the state of the Institution: "We have again the satisfaction to inform its friends and supporters, that the funds have received some considerable addition since the last year; and that the improvement in many of the patients, continues to be such, as to afford us encouragement in the undertaking.—Five patients have left the Institution since last year, so far recovered, as to render confinement unnecessary, though most of them were cases of long standing; several others are also much improved. Fifteen more patients have been admitted, in most of whom the disorder had existed for a considerable time; several of them had been removed from other Institutions of this nature, and considered as incurable. On this ground, the generality of them afford little or no prospect of a perfect recovery; yet divers of these appear more comfortable to themselves, and are improved in their mental faculties. There are now in the house 33 patients, viz. 16 men, and 17 women; eight of them at the low rate of four shillings per week, the rest from eight shillings to two guineas.

" The number of male patients having proved greater than was expected, an additional building has been undertaken, and is nearly completed; and also a separate piece of ground walled in for their accommodation.

" We find ourselves justified in the expectation we expressed last year, that the income from the patients, would be nearly sufficient for their support and attendance, as there appears a defect of only £14 : 8 : 1.

From the number now in the house, we hope that no deficiency on that account will, in future, take place."

The experience of the Retreat, had already proved the great importance of placing the insane under proper care, in an early stage of the disorder; and with a view of encouraging persons in straitened circumstances, to adopt this salutary measure, the general Meeting determined, " That in cases of derangement, not exceeding six months from their first appearance, those members of our society, whose circumstances, in case of continuance, would not conveniently admit of their paying more than 8*s*. per week; shall be entitled to an abatement of 4*s*. a week, for one year, if not sooner recovered. Those patients who, by the former rule, would have been rated at 4*s*. per week, will, under this regulation, be admitted gratis, for a year, if necessary."

From the Report brought to the General Meeting, in the 6th month, 1800, it appears that the addition to the property of the Institution this year, was £ 800 : 0 : 2; out of which the expense of the new building, £ 578 : 15 : 11, was defrayed.—The Report at this time, gives the following general view of the state of the Establishment:

" From the preceding statement, it appears, that the liberal contributions of Friends, have enabled the managers of the Institution, to discharge the expenses of the late additional building and furniture, besides which there is a small reduction of the debt. The very high price of provisions has frustrated the expectations which they formed last year, that the income from the patients would support the establishment, exclusive of the payment of life-annuities, and the interest of money borrowed.   The deficiency, however, does not amount to thirty pounds.

" Eleven patients have been admitted since the last year. Six have recovered, and been discharged ; three have died, two of whom were considerably advanced in years. There are at present in the house, 36 patients, viz. 15 men and 21 women; 11 of whom are at the low price of four shillings, and one at five shillings per week. Two patients, whose disorder was recent, and who formerly would have paid four shillings per week, were admitted gratis, in consequence of the agréement entered into last year. They are both recovered and discharged.

" Experience has this year abundantly convinced us, of the advantage to be derived from an early attention to persons afflicted with disorders of the mind. Of the eleven above reported to have been admitted, two were removed from another Institution, as incurables; and three others were confirmed cases. The remaining six were recent instances; four of whom recovered, and were discharged within the first quarter after their admission; the two others are evidently recovering, and will probably be dismissed within the same period. This consideration will, we hope, encourage the friends of those who are, or may be afflicted with this malady, to remove them early, and place them under proper care and treatment.

" We feel satisfaction in having it in our power to demonstrate the advantages of this Institution: and we trust that nothing now remains necessary to convince Friends of its utility, and to encourage them more generally to co-operate in its support."

The income from the patients, in the following year, reported in the 6th month, 1801, considerably exceeded the preceding; but, the expenses of the family, owing to the increased high price of provisions in this year, exceeded that income about £65. This deficiency was, however, more than compensated, by the liberality of the friends of the establishment; and

there was an increase of property this year, of
£ 145.

The Report of the General Meeting states: " There
have been thirteen patients admitted since the
last year.   Seven have been discharged in a state
of recovery ; and two have died.   The number now
in the house is 40 ; viz. 24 women and 16 men.   Besides the persons recovered, the condition of several
others has been so much meliorated, as to afford additional encouragement to those who have interested
themselves in this Institution.   Friends are now so
generally convinced of its utility, as to render it unnecessary to say much in its favour.   We indulge a
hope, that those who have not yet come forward in its
support, will be induced to unite with their friends
in this undertaking, as the debt with which it is still
encumbered, continues to claim the assistance of those
who feel for the afflictions of their fellow-creatures."

In this year, the Retreat was deprived, by death, of
the valuable services of Doctor Fowler, who had attended the Institution from its first opening; and
whose humane assiduity to relieve the unhappy objects of his care, had obtained for him the highest
esteem of the managers and family.

The Committee, in a conference with the subscribers of York, appointed Dr. Cappe his successor.

In making their Report, in the year 1802, the managers had the satisfaction to find, the hope was realized, which they had several times expressed, that the income arising from the patients, would be sufficient to defray the expenses of the family. There was a balance, this year, in favour of the latter, of £13:4:11; and there was, on the whole, an increase of property belonging to the Institution, of £45:5:3. This increase, however, arose chiefly from subscriptions for annuities, as the unconditional donations and legacies were much less than usual. But, as the annual subscriptions were, this year, considerably enlarged, it did not appear that the attention or interest of the Society, in regard to this Institution, was in any degree diminished; and the directors observe, at this time, in their Report: " We trust that the benefit resulting from it, will continue to attract the liberality of Friends, which yet remains necessary, for discharging the payments to annuitants, and the interest of money borrowed; as well as to effect the desirable object of gradually reducing the debt."

There were, at this time, in the house, thirteen men and twenty-nine women patients.

At the close of this year, the office of Physician again became vacant, by the death of Dr. Cappe; a man equally esteemed, for the gentle urbanity of his manners, the excellence of his understanding and dispositions, and his professional attainments. He bequeathed, in his will, several valuable books to the library of the Institution, by the following clause: " To the Retreat, as a token of my respect for that admirable Institution, I leave all my books and pamphlets treating solely on the disorders of the mind, or, in any way solely relative to that subject; as, descriptions of asylums, &c."

Dr. Belcombe, the present Physician, was appointed his successor, and we hope the Institution will long have the benefit of his valuable services.

Applications for admission still increased; and, the present accommodation being too small, it was agreed, in the 3d month, 1803, that an additional building should be erected, at the end of the west wing.

The income from the patients this year again exceeded the expenditure, and the property of the Institution experienced an increase of £258 : 16 : 3.

The Report states, "The number of patients admitted since the last year, is thirteen ; six have been discharged, either recovered or improved, and one has died. There are now forty-eight in the house, viz. seventeen men and thirty-one women."

In the years 1804 and 1805, the income arising from patients, rather exceeded the expenses of the family ; and there was an increase of property in these two years of £970, which fully defrayed the cost of the last new building. The average expense for each patient in the year 1804, was full £23 : 6 : 0 per annum.

The Reports were favourable as to the state of the patients, in proportion to the admissions ; only four being admitted in 1804, for want of room ; but in 1805, the number admitted was eleven. In these two years four died, and ten were discharged. Others were in a state of recovery, and it was believed that the situation of the whole was rendered as comfortable as their circumstances would admit.

In making up the accounts to the 3d month, 1806, it appeared that the expenditure exceeded the income

from the patients, £ 48 : 7 : 9; and that there was
a decrease in the property of the Institution, of
£ 39 : 12 : 3.   A very liberal and anonymous donation of £ 500, came in, very opportunely, about this
time ; and, in the following year, 1807, a favourable
statement of the Institution's finances, was again
presented ; by which there appeared an increase of
property, of £ 629 : 5 : 7.   The income from the
patients also exceeded the current expenses on their
account £ 24 : 11s.

In this and the preceding year, the number of
patients admitted, was twenty-one.   Four died, and
twelve were discharged, of whom ten were quite
recovered; and there were in the house, at the
time of each Report, fifty-three patients, viz. on the
average of the two years, twenty men and thirty-
three women.

The Report in the year 1808, again exhibited a
favourable account of the funds; and stated that
£ 675 had been subscribed for annuities, since the
last Report.   The managers, however, endeavoured to engage the attention of their friends by
stating, " that the Institution is now subject to the
payment of £136 : 5s. to annuitants, on the sum of

£2725; and there still remains a debt of £1859 : 17 : 8 owing for principal and interest."

In the course of the last year, fourteen patients were admitted, seven were discharged, recovered ; and one died. There were, at this time, fifty-nine patients in the house, viz. twenty-five men and thirty-four women.

The same number of patients were reported in the following year, 1809; but it was still found that the accommodations were inadequate to the wants of the Society. Several applications were rejected for want of room ; and it was, therefore, proposed to provide a separate house, to accommodate a few of those who might require the least extraordinary attention.

Ten patients had been admitted since the preceding annual Report : three had died, and seven had been taken away ; five of whom were recovered, and two removed to other situations on account of this house being too full. The income from the patients, again exceeded the expenditure, exclusive of the interest of money and the payments to annuitants; and the property of the Institution was increased £431 : 13 : 7.

The proposal to provide an additional house, was
acceded to at the Quarterly Meeting in the 9th
month; and an account was brought to the General
Meeting in the 6th month, 1810, that premises had
been purchased for the sum of £1200; and that a
few hundreds more would be required to make the
necessary alterations, and to furnish the house. The
Report published at this time stated, that as it was
desirable the debt already owing by the Institution,
should not be increased, a subscription had been
opened, and that £907:19s. had been offered towards
the additional accommodation proposed; but as that
sum was considerably short of the occasion, it was
hoped that other Friends would come forward with
contributions to supply the deficiency.

It also appeared, that from the very high price of provisions, the expenses of the family exceeded the income
received from the patients; and that the property
of the Institution was rather decreased. The Report
also states, " There have been five patients admitted
since last year; six have been taken away, recovered,
and two have died." The number of patients
remaining in the house, was fifty-seven, viz. twenty-
three men and thirty-four women.

In the year 1811, eight patients were reported as admitted, and seven discharged; of whom six were recovered, and the other much improved; one had died. The number remaining in the house, was the same as in the preceding year; with the variation of one in the proportion of the sexes, viz. twenty-four men and thirty-three women.

The Report in this year exhibited a very favourable view of the finances, and proved the esteem in which the Institution was generally held. Donations to the amount of £ 1399 : 4s. had been received on account of the Appendage; and a legacy of £ 500 had been bequeathed to the Institution. The income from patients this year, very nearly defrayed the expenses of the family; and the property of the Institution was increased £1779 : 4 : 3.

It is truly gratifying to observe the liberality with which this Institution has been hitherto supported by the Society; and I trust, if it continue to deserve their confidence, its funds will be yet more abundantly supplied.

The introductory part of the Report for the last year, I shall here insert.

" At a general Meeting of directors and subscribers,
held at York the 25th of 6th month, 1812, the Committee brought in the following Report:

" From the state of the accounts which is now laid
before the subscribers to this Institution, it will appear
that the expenditure on account of the patients, has
exceeded the income from them, to the amount of
£ 53 : 9 : 1; but this sum, considering all circumstances, and particularly the additional expenses of the
Appendage, is no more than might be expected. We
have, however, the satisfaction to state, that by means
of donations and legacies, this deficiency has not only
been supplied, but a surplus of £ 260 : 5 : 7 has ac-
crued in the property of the Institution, above the
total balance of the last year. It will be observed, that
a considerable sum on interest is still owing by the
Institution.

" There have been only six patients removed during
the last year; two of whom were recovered, and the
others improved.   Fifteen have been admitted, several
of whom were confirmed cases, and who had been
waiting some time till the Appendage was ready. None
have died this year.   There are now under the care of
the Institution, sixty-six patients, viz 26 men, and 40

women; of whom, four men, and eight women, are in the Appendage. This addition to the establishment, is found to be a great advantage to the Society, by admitting many patients, for whom accommodation was much wanted. It is, however, likely to occasion more expense than the income, from the increase of numbers, will defray. But for this, and for all other exigencies, we doubt not the liberality of Friends will sufficiently provide."

It will be seen by the statement of the accounts published in the year 1812, which concludes the summary of the finances, given in this chapter, that there is still a debt of £1745 : 10 : 10 for money borrowed, and interest upon it; and that the Institution remains liable also to the payment of £130 per annum for life-annuitants. If this debt were fully discharged, and the annual income materially increased, it is believed that several useful improvements might be made; and that an additional annual expenditure would promote the real welfare of the family.

I confess, however, I do not wish to see the Retreat wholly independent of annual contributions. The general interest which this mode of support naturally

F

occasions, and the constant stimulus which it must prove to those concerned in the management, to deserve the good opinion of the Society, cannot fail to have a salutary tendency.

This chapter will be closed, with the present rules for the government of the Institution ; but I wish, in concluding the present historical sketch of the Retreat, to congratulate those who have interested themselves in its establishment, on the satisfaction, which they must at present derive from the success of their benevolent exertions.

The necessity for such an establishment has, on every account, been found much greater than was at first imagined, and, in the degree in which it has contributed to the comforts of the unhappy objects of its care, it has equally exceeded the expectations of its most sanguine promoters.

A SUMMARY

OF THE

ANNUAL STATEMENTS OF THE FINANCES,

AS REPORTED

From the GENERAL MEETING of the DIRECTORS and SUBSCRIBERS,
referred to in page 48, and commencing

Sixth Month, 1797.

State of the Funds up to the 31st of 3d Month, 1797.

Property belonging to the Institution.

	£.	s.	d.
Land and improvements	1555	13	2
Buildings *	3869	16	8½
Furniture	506	12	11½
Cattle and provisions on hand	38	16	0
	£ 5970	18	10

Debts owing by the Institution.

	£.	s.	d.
To sundry persons on interest	1945	0	0
Interest due thereon	19	14	8
Half a year due to annuitants	20	12	6
To patients' time unexpired	24	11	8
Owing on account of buildings	911	13	7
Ditto on land account	2	19	6
Ditto on furniture account	11	9	10
To W. Tuke, as treasurer	365	15	2½
	3301	16	11½
Balance in favour of the Institution	2669	1	10½
	£ 5970	18	10

* The buildings include the Cold Bath, and divers additional buildings not in
the first plan and estimate.

F 2

N. B. The Institution also remains subject to the payment of 5 per cent. per annum to life annuitants, on the sum of £825.

	£.	s.	d.
House expenses from 1st of 6th month, 1796, to 1st of 4th month, 1797	316	13	0½
Income from the patients	212	1	0
Expenditure above the income	104	12	0½

Report, Sixth Month, 1798.

	£.	s.	d.
Income from the patients	388	9	10
Donations	433	14	6
Annual subscriptions	40	19	0
Subscription for an annuity	100	0	0
A contingency	2	10	0
	965	13	4

	£.	s.	d.
House expenses, including salaries and servants' wages, cultivation of the land, &c.	434	0	0
Linen, wear and tear	15	0	0
Furniture, ditto	25	10	0
Physician and medicine	39	2	10
Extra expenses	6	17	10
	520	10	8

	£.	s.	d.	
Interest of money borrowed	135	1	5	
Ditto to annuitants	41	15	6	
			176	16 11
			697	7 7
Increase of property			£268	5 9

Sixth Month, 1799.

	£.	s.	d.
Income from the patients	878	9	0½
Donations and annual subscriptions	449	12	6
Total income	1128	1	6½

	£.	s.	d.			
Expenses of the Institution	692	17	1½			
Annuitants and interest of money	190	3	3½	883	0	5
Increase of property				245	1	1½

Sixth Month, 1800.

	£.	s.	d.
Income from the patients	863	16	3½
Legacies, donations, annual subscriptions, and subscriptions for annuities*	1032	11	0
Total income	1896	7	3½

	£.	s.	d.			
Expenses of the establishment	£887	14	1½			
Annuities and int. of money borrowed	208	13	0	1096	7	1½
Increase of property,				£800	0	2

Which was chiefly expended in new buildings.

Sixth Month, 1801.

	£.	s.	d.	£.	s.	d.
Income from the patients	997	14	0			
Contributions	416	2	0	1413	16	0
Expenses of the establishment	1062	14	9¼			
Annuities and int. of money borrowed	205	11	0	1268	5	9½
Increase of property				£ 145	10	2½

* As these particulars comprise all the usual modes of aiding the funds of this Institution, it is not thought needful to particularise them in the future summaries of receipts; nor does it appear necessary to repeat the items of expenditure, given in the two or three first annual statements.

F 3

Sixth Month, 1802.

	£.	s.	d.	£.	s.	d.
Income from the patients	1082	11	11			
Contributions	239	18	0			
				1322	9	11
Expenses of the establishment	1069	6	11½			
Annuities and int. of money borrowed	207	17	8			
				1277	4	7½
Increase of property				£45	5	3½

Sixth Month, 1803.

	£.	s.	d.	£.	s.	d.
Income from the patients	1114	10	3½			
Contributions	388	0	0			
				1502	10	3½
Expenses of the establishment . ..	1029	5	10½			
Annuities and int. of money borrowed	214	8	2			
				1243	14	0½
Increase of property				£258	16	3

Sixth Month, 1804.

	£.	s.	d.	£.	s.	d.
Income from the patients	1191	16	8¼			
Contributions	595	5	6			
				1787	2	2½
Expenses of the establishment	1126	10	3			
Annuities and int. of money borrowed	211	9	1			
				1337	19	4
Increase of property				£449	2	10½

Sixth Month, 1805.

	£.	s.	d.	£.	s.	d.
Income from the patients	1146	11	4			
Ditto, arising from the decease of a patient, for whose maintenance a sum of money had been sunk ...	391	5	0			
Contributions	379	0	0			
				1916	16	4
Expenses of the establishment	1189	16	3			
Annuities and int. of money borrowed	205	13	11			
				1395	10	2
Increase this year				£ 521	6	2

Sixth Month, 1806.

	£.	s.	d.	£.	s.	d.
Expenses of the establishment	1325	9	1½			
Annuities and int. of money borrowed	220	1	6			
				1545	10	7½
Income from the patients	1277	1	4			
Contributions	228	17	0			
				1505	18	4
Decrease of property				£ 39	12	3½

Sixth Month, 1807.

	£.	s.	d.	£.	s.	d.
Income from patients	1301	18	6			
Contributions	821	12	6			
				2123	11	0
Expenses of the establishment	1277	7	6			
Annuities and int. of money borrowed	216	17	11			
				1494	5	5
Increase of property				£ 629	5	7

Sixth Month, 1808.

	£.	s.	d.	£.	s.	d.
Income from the patients	1355	19	9			
Contributions, chiefly for annuities ..	877	9	0			
				2233	8	9
Expenses of the establishment	1335	4	10½			
Annuities and int. of money borrowed	207	18	6			
				1543	3	4½
Increase this year				£ 690	5	4½

Sixth Month, 1809.

	£.	s.	d.	£.	s.	d.
Income from the patients	1592	18	7			
Contributions	585	15	0			
				2178	13	7
Expenses of the Institution	1535	6	6			
Annuities and int. of money borrowed	211	13	6			
				1747	0	0
Increase of property				£ 431	13	7

Sixth Month, 1810.

	£.	s.	d.	£.	s.	d.
Expenses of the establishment	1640	18	3½			
Annuities and int. of money borrowed	204	4	4			
				1845	2	7½
Income from patients	1590	1	9			
Contributions	210	5	0			
				1800	6	9
Decrease this year				£ 44	15	10½

Sixth Month, 1811.

	£.	s.	d.	£.	s.	d.
Income from the patients	1615	0	8			
Contributions	1992	5	0			
				3607	5	8
Expenses of the establishment	1618	12	10½			
Annuities and int. of money borrowed	209	8	6			
				1828	1	4½

Increase, principally in consequence of the addition of the Appendage £1779 4 3½

Sixth Month, 1812.

INCOME.

	£.	s.	d.
Income from patients	1828	4	11
Donations	161	10	6
Annual Subscriptions	47	5	0
Legacies £350 0 0			
Duty deducted 35 0 0	315	0	0
Total income	2352	0	5

EXPENDITURE.

	£.	s.	d.
House expenses	1218	5	6
Ditto Appendage	181	0	11
Linen, wear and tear	22	8	9
Furniture, ditto	55	14	0
Salaries and Servants' Wages, Physician's included	318	0	0
Ditto Appendage	12	13	0
Drugs	14	17	0
Repairs and extra expenses	58	14	10
Expenses of the establishment	1881	14	0

	£.	s.	d.
Expenses of the establishment brought over	1881	14	0
Interest of Money	77	2	6
Annuities	132	18	4
Total expenditure	2091	14	10
Increase of property	260	5	7
Income, as before stated	£2352	0	5

PROPERTY BELONGING TO THE INSTITUTION.

	£.	s.	d.
Land and improvements	1633	0	0
Buildings	5831	7	8
Appendage, purchase and improvements	1765	0	8
Linen	127	3	0
Ditto, at the Appendage	39	1	7
Furniture	1034	16	0
Ditto, at the Appendage	264	2	4
Provisions on hand	226	16	5
Drugs	7	0	0
Patients, due from them	581	13	8
	£11510	1	4

DEBTS OWING BY THE INSTITUTION.

	£.	s.	d.
To sundry persons, principal and interest	1745	10	10
To annuitants	115	0	0
For Salaries and Servants' Wages	174	6	0
Balance due to William Tuke	354	10	6
Balance in favour of the Institution	9120	14	0
	£11510	1	4

☞ The Institution also remains subject to the payment of five per cent. per annum to life-annuitants, on the sum of £2600.

Total of Subscriptions of Friends within each Quarterly Meeting, to the 6th month, 1812.

	Donations.			Annuities.
	£.	s.	d.	£.
Bedfordshire and Hertfordshire	182	0	0	100
Berks and Oxfordshire	56	17	6	
Bristol and Somersetshire	537	19	0	200
Buckinghamshire	127	19	6	
Cambridgeshire and Huntingdonshire ..	108	16	6	50
Cheshire	6	1	6	
Cornwall	58	6	0	
Cumberland and Northumberland	62	16	6	
Devonshire	20	10	0	
Durham	108	18	0	100
Derbyshire and Nottinghamshire	133	12	0	
Essex	120	5	0	400
Gloucestershire and Wilts	251	8	0	
Herefordshire and Worcestershire	110	0	0	
Kent	1	1	0	
Lancashire	296	0	6	200
Lincolnshire	56	15	6	
London and Middlesex	1099	13	6	900
Norfolk and Norwich	101	0	0	
Northamptonshire	25	15	0	
Suffolk	300	8	0	150
Surrey and Sussex	166	4	0	
Scotland	34	2	6	
Wales	400	0	0	
Warwickshire, &c.	172	3	0	
Westmoreland	66	1	6	
Yorkshire	1408	5	6	725
Ireland ....,.................	0	0	0	100
Rhode Island	20	0	0	
Anonymous	694	2	0	
Legacies	1995	16	0	
Total	£8722	17	6	2925

FORM OF A BEQUEST.

I give and bequeath to the treasurer, for the time being, of an Institution, near York, called, " The Retreat for persons afflicted with disorders of the mind, among the Society of Friends," *the sum of*

to be paid out of my personal estate, and applied towards carrying on the benevolent designs of that Institution.

RULES AND REGULATIONS.

SECTION I.

CONTRIBUTIONS.

1st. THE Institution was established by annuities, donations, and annual subscriptions; by means of which, and the addition of legacies, it continues to be supported; and the same may be further promoted amongst Friends, within the compass of any Quarterly Meeting.

2d. Each Subscriber, by way of annuity, contributing a sum of not less than twenty pounds, shall receive an interest of five per cent. per annum during life.

3d. A contribution of one hundred pounds, from any Quarterly or other Meeting in its collective capacity; a donation of twenty-five pounds from any Friend; or a subscription of fifty pounds for an annuity, shall entitle such meeting, donor, or annuitant, respectively, to the privilege of nominating one poor patient at a time, on the lowest terms of admission.

4th. In consideration of the smallness of a Quarterly Meeting, or of its members not being in an eligible situation to raise one hundred pounds, the General Meeting of subscribers shall have power, on application, to extend the privilege of the third rule to such Meetings, on contributing a smaller sum, at the discretion of the said General Meeting.

5th. The privilege of Meetings, or of persons to recommend poor patients on the lowest terms of admission, according to the third and fourth rules, shall not be taken away or diminished, notwithstanding any general powers which are, or may be invested in the future directors.

6th. As it is necessary to ascertain the subscriptions of each meeting, that may have a right to recommend poor patients, donors of twenty-five pounds and upwards, are desired to explain, whether they wish to enjoy the privilege, during life, of recommending poor patients, or that their donations should be considered as the subscriptions of their Quarterly or other Meetings : and it is agreed, that all donations of individuals, not claiming such right of recommendation, shall be considered as a subscription of their Quarterly Meeting, whether reported to such Meeting, or not ; and every Quarterly Meeting shall enjoy the privilege of recommending poor patients, in proportion to the subscription of their respective members.

7th. The name when sent up, of every annuitant, donor, and subscriber, shall be recorded in a book kept for that purpose ; and every annuitant, donor of not less than two guineas, and subscriber of sums in any manner equal to two guineas, being and continuing a member of our Society, shall be a member of the meetings, which are to be held for the government and superintendence of the Institution.

8th. For the satisfaction of Subscribers on life-annuities, and those who have lent, or may hereafter lend, any money to this Institution, this Meeting declares, that the whole real and personal property thereunto belonging, acquired, and to be acquired, shall stand and continue a security to the said life-annuitants, for the annual payment of their interests, and to the lenders aforesaid, for the regular payment of principal and interest.

SECTION II.

GOVERNMENT.

1st. A General Meeting shall be held in the latter end of the 6th month, or the beginning of the 7th month of every year, unless some other time should hereafter be found more convenient. The Friends who may compose it, shall, from time to time, have a general state of the family, and accounts of the Institution, laid before them; and, except the two minutes which relate to securities to annuitants, to lenders of money, and to privileged meetings and subscribers, shall have power to alter or make rules, and give such directions, as they may think best adapted to promote the designs of the Institution; and to appoint a treasurer, who shall keep and dispose of the money entrusted to him, as the said Meeting shall direct. They may also confirm, alter, or abrogate, the orders and regulations of the Quarterly Meetings; and shall choose annually a Committee for the immediate care and management of the undertaking. This Committee are to meet once a month, or oftener if necessary; fix the terms of admission for the different patients; make out clear and distinct accounts

of the state of the Institution; and carry into execution the rules and orders made for promoting its
welfare*.

2d. During, or after the conclusion of, each
Quarterly Meeting of Friends for Yorkshire, a Meeting
is to be held, to receive a Report of the said Committee's accounts, read over all their minutes, advance
or reduce the weekly payment of any of the patients,
and give the Committee such advice and direction as
they may think proper; consistently with the general
rules and orders that may have been established.

3d. The General Meeting in the year 1800, according to the original plan of the Institution, made
provision for a perpetual succession of Directors.
Forty subscribers, members of our Society, were
nominated and appointed, who, with their successors,
as hereafter directed to be appointed, together with
any other donors or subscribers, qualified according
to the third rule of Section 1st; and agents that
may be appointed by any qualified Meeting, which
may from time to time choose to attend, are to be

---

* This Committee appoints three female visiters, one of whom is
changed every month.

G

the General Meeting; and to continue the Directors of the Institution; in whom the government of it is perpetually to vest and remain; and ten of whom are to be sufficient to do business. The said forty Directors, or any eight of them, with any other qualified donors or subscribers, are to meet quarterly for the purposes of the preceding rule.

4th. At the expiration of each year, the first named eight on the list, are to cease to be Directors; and eight other members of our Society, are to be appointed by the General Meeting in their place; with an addition for such as may be deceased or disowned. Any Directors may be chosen from the number of donors and subscribers, or others, as shall, in process of time, be judged most convenient and best.

5th. If at any future period, by means of some unforeseen or unexpected events, it should appear to the General Meeting, that the original purpose of the undertaking, cannot be accomplished or pursued, the said General Meeting shall give due notice in writing to all the Directors, and also in every Quarterly or other Meeting of our Society, which according to the rules, may be interested therein.

that the disposal of the property of the Institution is
to be taken under consideration at their next Meeting.
At such Meeting, two agents or representatives, appointed by any of the said Meetings, shall be admitted as Members of the General Meeting. In case
two-thirds of the Meeting so convened shall agree
thereto, they may sell or dispose of the whole estate
and property of the Institution, or of any part thereof,
or appropriate the same, or the neat produce thereof,
to such just, equitable, or charitable uses, as they,
on serious and deliberate consideration, shall judge
best.

SECTION III.

PATIENTS.

1st. The terms for board, washing, medical advice,
and medicines, and all other things necessary, except
clothing, are, for every poor patient privileged agreeably to the third rule, a sum not less than four
shillings per week.

2d. Not less than eight shillings per week shall
be paid for other patients, and more according to
circumstances; and a reasonable sum for the board

of the servant of any patient, whose friends should incline to send one; which servant must be approved by the Committee. The terms of admission to be subject to future alteration, if found necessary ; and, as the wearing of washing gowns and skirts is at present so much increased, that the washing of them in so large a family is attended with considerable inconvenience, it is agreed, that those belonging to the patients, shall be washed out of the house, and the expense charged to their respective accounts.

3d. A quarter of a year's maintenance for each patient, is to be paid in advance; and in case the patient should be cured, or die before the expiration of the first quarter, no part thereof is to be returned; but, after the first quarter, return is to be made for the number of whole weeks unexpired, at the time of removal, or decease of a patient.

4th. As experience demonstrates, that the recovery of insane patients, frequently depends on their being removed from their connexions, and put under proper care and treatment, in the early stages of the disorder, it is earnestly recommended to their friends, to remove them at an early period after the disorder appears to be fixed. And, as an additional inducement to persons in straitened circumstances, to adopt this salutary measure, it is concluded, that in derangements not exceeding six months from their first appearance, those Members of our Society, whose circumstances, in case of continuance, would not conveniently admit of their paying more than eight shillings per week, shall be entitled to an abatement of four shillings a week for one year, if not sooner recovered. Those patients who, by the former rule, would have been rated at four shillings per week, will, under this regulation, be admitted gratis for a year, if necessary : But, as some patients have come with disorders unconnected with insanity, and which require additional expense or attendance, it is judged necessary, that, in such cases, an additional charge shall be made, at the discretion of the Committee.

5th. On the admission of patients, the Committee should, in general, require a certificate signed by a medical person, to the following import ; *I do hereby certify, that A. B. of C, aged —— years, is in a state of insanity, and proper to be received into a house provided for the relief of persons of that description.* It should also be stated, whether the patient is afflicted with any complaint independent of insanity. It is also desirable, that some account should be sent, how

long the patient has been disordered ; whether any,
or what sort of medical means have been used ; and
whether any disposition has appeared in the patient
to injure him or herself, or any other person : with
any other circumstances likely to throw light on the
case relative to his or her treatment.

6th. As the Committee is not to admit any patient,
on lower terms than eight shillings per week, unless
recommended by the agent of a privileged Meeting,
or by a subscriber qualified according to the third
rule respecting contributions, it is hoped that individual subscribers, will be cautious of recommending
patients, whose maintenance, or any part thereof, is
paid by a monthly or other Meeting, to the saving of
the expense of the members of such Meetings col-
lectively ; thereby rendering it unnecessary for them
to subscribe to the Institution : But no discourage-
ment is hereby intended, to the assistance of Friends
whose circumstances, or those of their near connexions, are too strait to pay eight shillings per week.

7th. As, in many cases, it may be difficult for the
friends of patients to procure suitable persons to conduct them to the house, it is agreed that, on application, a proper person shall be sent from the Retreat,

when it is convenient; the expenses only being paid by the patients' friends.

8th. Though it was the original design of this Institution, to accommodate such insane persons only, as are members of our Society; yet it was also considered that cases might arise, wherein it might be desirable to extend such accommodation beyond the line of strict membership; but as an indiscriminate admittance of persons not in membership, would defeat the special design of the Institution, by the exclusion of those who are members, the admitting, or not admitting of them, must always be left to the discretion of the Committee, and consequently time given for consideration.

9th. The sending of patients without previous application, should, in all cases, be avoided, lest suitable accommodation be not at liberty for their reception; and Friends should also avoid bringing patients at late hours of the night.

10th. As circumstances may sometimes occur, wherein it is proper that the Committee should have a discretion to decline the admission of patients, though members of our Society; especially when the house is nearly full ; it is agreed to vest such discretion in the Committee, until the Quarterly or General Meeting can be consulted ; which Meeting shall determine the propriety of admitting or refusing such applications.

N. B. There are apartments in which patients with a servant may be accommodated, without mixing with the others.

CHAPTER III.

DESCRIPTION AND APPROPRIATION OF THE GROUNDS AND HOUSE.

*Situation———General aspect of the Building———
The Farm———The Garden———The Courts for the
different classes of Patients———Remarks———Application of the different parts of the Building to the
use of the Patients———On attention to the comfort
of the Insane———The Retreat not a perfect model
for erections of this kind———Early Managers laboured
under the want of experience———The advantages of
the Building described———Of its defects.———Of the
excessive attention to safety in the construction of
Hospitals for the Insane.*

THE Retreat is situate on an eminence, at the
distance of about half a mile from the eastern gate
of the city of York. It commands a very delightful
prospect, extending, on the south, as far as the eye
can reach, over a wooded, fertile plain; and termina-
ting on the north and east, by the Hambleton Hills
and the Wolds; which are seen, in some places, at
the distance of about twenty-five miles.

The situation combines nearly all the circumstances, which are usually considered favourable to longevity; and the almost uniform health of the family, has confirmed the general observations on this subject.

In the erection of the building, which is of brick, economy and convenience have been chiefly consulted. Dr. Delarive describes the general appearance as being that of a rural farm; but, I confess, I cannot see the resemblance. The size of the panes of glass, certainly denies it the character of the modern mansion; at the same time, that the absence of bars before the windows, and the garden in front being defended from the road, only by a neat common hedge, prevent, entirely, the aspect of a place of confinement.

There are eleven acres of land belonging to the Institution. This little farm is chiefly occupied in the growth of potatoes, and the support of the cows, which supply the family with milk and butter.

The garden is on the north side of the house, and contains about one acre. This furnishes abundance of fruit and vegetables. It also affords an agreeable

GROUND PLAN of the RETREAT near YORK.

place for recreation and employment, to many of the patients; being divided by gravel-walks, interspersed with shrubs and flowers, and sheltered from the intrusive eye of the passenger, by a narrow plantation and shrubberry.

On the south side of the house, as will be seen in the plan, are the courts for the different classes of patients. The circular wall which encloses the male and female patients' courts, marked No. 1 on the ground plan, are about eight feet high; but, as the ground declines from the house, their apparent height is not so great; and the view from them of the country is consequently not so much obstructed, as it would be if the ground was level. I cannot, however, forbear observing, that the courts appear to be too small, and to admit of too little variety, to invite the patient to take exercise. The boundary of his excursion is always before his eye; which must have a gloomy effect on the already depressed mind. This might be considered as a serious defect, if it was not generally compensated, by taking such patients as are suitable, into the garden; and by frequent excursions into the city or the surrounding country, and into the fields of the Institution. One of these is surrounded by a walk, interspersed with trees and shrubs.

The superintendent has also endeavoured to furnish a source of amusement, to those patients whose walks are necessarily more circumscribed, by supplying each of the courts with a number of animals; such as rabbits, sea-gulls, hawks, and poultry. These creatures are generally very familiar with the patients : and it is believed they are not only the means of innocent pleasure ; but that the intercourse with them, sometimes tends to awaken the social and benevolent feelings.

The plans which are given of the building, will afford a correct idea of its extent; but the reader will probably wish to be informed, of the appro-priation of its different parts, to the use of the patients.

It will be proper first to mention, that there are, at present, under the care of the Institution, twenty-four male and thirty-eight female patients ; but, of these, four men and seven women are in the building at some distance, distinguished by the name of the Appendage. These patients are of the confirmed class, and are such as do not, in general, require extraordinary coercion.

There are two day-rooms in the Retreat, on the ground floor, which are occupied by the men patients. The day-room in the extreme east building, and the court adjoining to it No. 2, are occupied by the more violent patients, and such as are least capable of rational enjoyment. The number of patients in this room varies; but is usually from seven to ten. They are under the general care of one attendant; who also prepares the room for their reception in the morning, brings them their meals, and makes their beds. In his several offices, he is frequently assisted by some of those, who are under his care.

The windows in this room are small, double sashes, of cast iron, placed at four feet and a quarter from the ground, and are not defended by any grating. This is not found necessary, although on an average there are not more than two male patients, under any personal restraint by arm-straps, jacket, &c. The patients are prevented from approaching too near the fire, by a circular iron guard. This projects about three feet and a half, is enclosed at the top, and opens in front by a small door, which is kept locked.

An apartment near this day-room is used, when necessary, for the entire seclusion of a violent patient. It is furnished with a bed, securely fastened to the ground. Light is, in great measure, but not entirely excluded; and care is taken to have the room properly ventilated.

This room also affords an opportunity of temporary confinement, by way of punishment, for any very offensive acts, which it is thought the patient had the power to restrain; but this very rarely occurs; and I am happy to say, the apartment is frequently unoccupied; or in other words, there is not, on an average, from any cause, one male patient in a state of seclusion during the day.

The day-room in the east wing, adjoining the parlour, and the male patients' court No. 1, accommodate the superior class, in regard to behaviour, and to capacity of rational enjoyment. There are two windows in the room, which afford an agreeable view of the country. They are three feet and a half wide by six feet high, each containing 48 panes of glass, or 24 in each sash. The frames of the sashes are of cast iron, about one inch and a half square; the glass-bars are about five-eighths of an inch thick, and each pane of glass is about six inches and a half by seven and a half. Air is admitted through the windows, by placing the upper cast iron sash, not glazed, immediately over the lower one, and hanging a glazed wooden sash, precisely of the same dimensions, on the outside of the iron frame. In this manner the double sash windows, in general, especially in the patients' apartments, are all effectually secured, without an appearance of any thing more than common sashes with small squares. It is not found necessary here, in general, to protect the fire by a guard, as in the other day-room. The number of patients in this room, who are intrusted to one attendant, is at present twelve. The offices are similar to those of the attendant, in the other day-room.

Patients of the higher class, in regard to property, and who can be intrusted to leave the gallery, take their meals with the superintendent and the female patients of the same class, in the dining-room, of the centre building. The convalescents of the lower class, many of whom have been, previously to their disorder, in respectable situations, are frequently admitted to take their meals in this room; as the change is found essentially to promote their recovery.

All the lodging-rooms on the ground floor, and those of the second story, in the extreme east building, are appropriated to male patients. The general size of the windows in these rooms, is three feet by three feet six inches. They are placed between six and seven feet from the floor, and reach to the ceiling; the height of each room, being about nine feet. Many of these windows were originally boarded up, except one row of panes; but experience has proved this precaution to be generally unnecessary; and the shutters are most of them removed. The frames of the sashes are of cast iron, as already described page 98; but these windows being only a single sash, air is admitted at the upper row of panes, consisting of six squares, by not glazing one half, and having a small wooden slide, with three panes of glass in it, to open and shut as occasion requires. Air is also admitted into the patients' rooms through a small wicket in the door, which is thus constructed: The door has six flat pannels, and the two upper ones have a small wicket between them, hung with two joints on one edge, and bevelled on the other edge to prevent its passing through. Thus, when shut, it is even with the pannels. Over the wicket, slides, in a groove, a piece that completes the appearance of the munnion, or middle

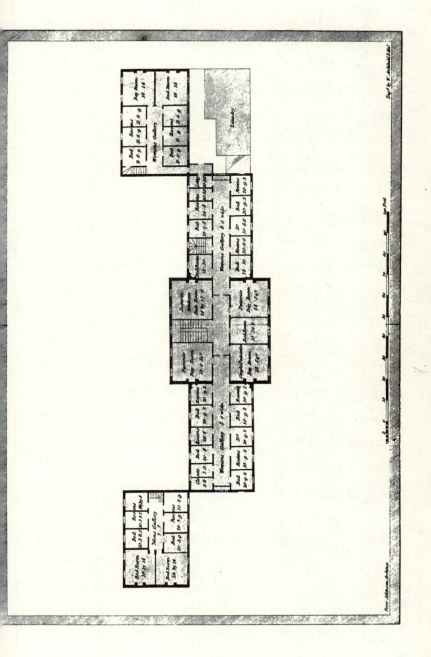

PLAN of the SECOND FLOOR of the RETREAT near YORK.

Eng'd by V. ARRASMITH

stile of the door; and when this is in its usual place, it leaves no appearance different from that of a common door. This contrivance not only admits air, for ventilation, but affords an opportunity for the attendants, quietly to look in, if a patient's situation requires such attention. Each door is secured by a small, spring, mortice lock; and also a bolt on the outside: but the grating sound of the latter, is very objectionable; and it appears that a strong, spring, mortice lock, would afford sufficient security in all cases.

The furniture in the bed-rooms varies, according to the terms upon which the patient is admitted, and to his state of mind. The bedsteads of that class of patients, who are insensible to the usual calls of nature, have circular wood bottoms, perforated with holes; beneath which is placed a receiver. The bed is merely clean straw, over which is laid a blanket; upon this the patient sleeps, and is covered with blankets. The other patients, of whatever rank, have the usual kind of beds or mattrasses. The beds of those who are not of the lowest class, are of better quality. They are half-headed, and furnished with curtains, put up in so slight a manner, as to prevent the possibility of any danger arising from this indulgence.

H

An air of neatness and comfort is thus given to the
rooms; and, though some have been disposed to
contemn as superfluous the attention paid to the lesser
feelings of the patients, there is great reason to believe, it has been of considerable advantage.

The "single patient's day-room," and the chamber
adjoining, in the front of the centre building, on the
second story, are occupied by a male patient who
has a distinct attendant. These rooms would not
be ineligible for the accommodation of a person in
any rank of life.

The other three day-rooms on the second story,
are occupied by female patients. The more re-
fractory class usually occupy that in the extreme
west building, and the " female patients' court,
No. 2." There are upon the ground floor, two
rooms for the entire seclusion of patients during the
day, when necessary. These, however, like that
appropriated to the same class of male patients, are
very frequently unoccupied; and, on an average,
there is not one female patient, requiring solitary confinement during the day. The number in the day-room
assigned to the worst class, is generally from ten to
twelve. The other day-rooms, are not occupied by

distinct classes of patients, either in regard to circumstances, or to state of mind; except that if a patient
finds the society in one room unpleasant, she is removed to the other. Each of these rooms has a
female attendant or nurse, who, with the assistance
of some of the convalescents, does every thing for
the patients under her care, except preparing their
food. The windows are double sashes, undefended
by any grating, as already described. The fires in
all the female patients' day-rooms, are at present
protected by guards.

There are about five or six patients of the superior
class, both in respect of terms and disorder, who
occupy the dining-room as a day-room. The bed-
rooms of this class, are in the attic of the centre
building; and nothing particular appears in the
manner of the furniture; though the curtains are not
hung upon rods as usual; but are slightly attached
to the head of the bed. These chambers are very comfortable, and the prospect from them is most delightful:
one of them is used as a day-room, by a patient who
has a distinct attendant. The windows are double
sashes; and are placed at the usual height from
the floor. The doors are secured by the spring
locks.

H 2

The attention which is due to the comfort of the insane, and the degree in which it is compatible with their security, appear to have been, till very recently, objects of little general consideration. It is not, therefore, to be supposed, that the Retreat, which has now been erected seventeen years, and which was originally intended for only thirty patients, should be a perfect model for establishments of this kind; though every care was exercised in its first construction. Indeed, it is hardly probable, as the class of persons, both as to rank and disease, in different establishments, must be various, that the arrangements in any one, can be precisely followed in another.

The promoters of this Institution, as they observed in one of their early Reports, could not be supposed to be superior to those disadvantages, to which the want of experience naturally exposed them. When it is also considered, that they were unable to form any probable opinion, of the proportions of the different classes of patients, either in regard to rank or disease; and that the number has, unhappily, so much exceeded their expectations, it will not be surprising, that the building has several imperfections; but rather that it possesses so many advantages.

It has been already observed, that the aspect of a
place of confinement is prevented, by the substitution
of cast iron window frames for the bars, which, in
similar places, usually guard the avenues of light.
This contrivance unites the advantages of security,
neatness, and durability.   There are not in this house
any cells under ground.   All the rooms, except three
which derive their light from an adjoining gallery,
have glass windows.   Iron bars and shutters, are too
often substituted for glazed windows, in rooms appropriated to the insane.   The obvious consequence
is, that the air, however cold, cannot be kept out of
the apartment, without the entire exclusion of
light.

The distance at which the lodging-room windows
are placed from the ground, is, in many instances,
a necessary precaution, to prevent the injury of the
patient, or the destruction of glass.   There has not,
however, appeared occasion for this precaution, to
the extent in which it seems to have been anticipated ;
and it would perhaps be better, if, in a few more of
the gallery lodging-rooms, the windows would allow
the patient to view the surrounding country.   It
may be proper to observe, that, in the galleries,
each patient lodges in a distinct apartment.

H 3

One circumstance, which I much regret, in the construction of this building, is, that there are rooms on both sides of the galleries; for, though a large portion of light is admitted, by the window at each extremity of the building, yet, the galleries on the ground floor, at least, are rather gloomy.

I observe with pleasure, in a very ingenious account and plan of a new asylum at Glasgow*, that the galleries have rooms on one side, and windows on the other. This cannot fail to give an air of cheerfulness, highly desirable in such establishments.

Many errors in the construction, as well as in the management of asylums for the insane, appear to arise from excessive attention to *safety*. People, in general, have the most erroneous notions of the constantly outrageous behaviour, or malicious dispositions, of deranged persons; and it has, in too many instances, been found convenient to encourage

---

* " Remarks on the Construction of Public Hospitals," by Wm. Stark, Esq. architect. This work, as well as " Observations on the Treatment of Lunatics," by Robert Reid, Esq. architect, deserves the attention of those who are engaged in such undertakings.

these false sentiments, to apologize for the treatment of the unhappy sufferers, or admit the vicious
neglect of their attendants *.

In the construction of such places, cure and comfort ought to be as much considered, as security ;
and, I have no hesitation in declaring, that a system
which, by limiting the power of the attendant, obliges
him not to neglect his duty, and makes it his interest
to obtain the good opinion of those under his care,
provides more effectually for the safety of the keeper,
as well as of the patient, than all " the apparatus of
chains, darkness, and anodynes."

---

* I once accidentally visited a house for insane persons, in which
security was made a *primary* object. Here I saw three of the
keepers, in the middle of the day, earnestly employed in—*playing
at cards !*

H 4

Since several sheets of this work were printed off, inquiries have been made, which induces us to supply, in this place, the accidental omission, in the second chapter, of

AN ACCOUNT OF THE FAMILY ESTABLISHMENT.

———◆———

Superintendent and apothecary ......George Jepson.

Female Superintendent ......Katharine Jepson.

Assistant to ditto.

Two male attendants.

One ditto, on a single patient.

Three female attendants.

One ditto, on a single patient.

Cook, and a girl to assist.

Laundry-maid.

An assistant to ditto, and to the nurses or female attendants.

One labourer.

One man who brews, bakes, &c. and, with the labourer, works in the garden.

———————

A gardener is occasionally employed.

CHAPTER IV.

MEDICAL TREATMENT.

Character of the first Physician——Result of his experiments as to the general importance of Medical treatment——Of the reducing system in particular—— Of forcing the Patient to take medicine——Consequent humane direction of the Physician——Of the use of the Warm Bath in Melancholia——In Mania—— Mode of using it——Use of Cold Bath in a case of high Mania——Importance of attention to the general health of the Insane——Frequent extraordinary sympathy between body and mind in this class of persons——Advantage of attention to the bodily health of Convalescents——Use of topical bleeding on the approach of a paroxysm——Necessity of close individual attention to Patients, an argument against large Establishments——Difficulty of obtaining Sleep——Mode practised at the Retreat—— Want of discrimination in the medical treatment of Insanity——Remarks on the practice of Bethlem Hospital——Of mortifications of the extremities from cold or confinement——Of the capacity of Maniacs to bear cold——Of Diet——

Usual bill of fare——Of the antiphlogistic system——
Doubt respecting the Diet of the Retreat——Of the
capacity of Maniacs to bear hunger——Beneficial
effects of air and exercise.

THE experience of the Retreat, if it should contribute in some degree to the improvement, will not
add much to the honour or extent of medical science.
I regret that it will be the business of the present
chapter, to relate the pharmaceutic means which
have failed, rather than to record those which
have succeeded.

The physician * first appointed to attend at the
Retreat, was a man equally distinguished by medical
knowledge, and indefatigable perseverance. He
possessed too, (which rendered him peculiarly adapted
to the place he filled,) a highly benevolent and unprejudiced mind. His experience had not been
great in that particular branch of his profession,
which on this occasion claimed his attention; but,
as might be expected, he entered on his office with
the anxiety and ardour of a feeling mind, upon the

---

* Dr. Thomas Fowler, author of " Medical Reports," &c. &c.

exertion of whose skill, depended the dearest interests
of many of his fellow-creatures. He determined to
give a full trial of the means, which his own judgment
might suggest, or which the superior knowledge and
experience of others had already recommended.
But the sanguine expectations, which he successively
formed of benefit to be derived from various pharmaceutic remedies, were, in great measure, as successively disappointed; and, although the proportion
of cures, in the early part of the Institution, was
respectable; yet the medical means were so im-
perfectly connected with the progress of recovery,
that he could not avoid suspecting them, to be
rather concomitants than causes. Further experiments and observations confirmed his suspicions;
and led him to the painful conclusion, (painful alike
to our pride and to our humanity,) that medicine,
as yet, possesses very inadequate means to relieve
the most grievous of human diseases.

Bleeding, blisters, seatons, evacuants, and many
other prescriptions, which have been highly recommended by writers on insanity, received an ample
trial; but they appeared to the physician too ineffica-
cious, to deserve the appellation of remedies, except
when indicated by the general state of the habit. As

the use of antimaniacal medicines was thus doubtful, a very strong argument against them arose, from the difficulty with which they were very frequently administered; as well as from the impossibility of employing powerful medicines, in a long continuance, without doing some injury to the constitution. The physician plainly perceived how much was to be done by moral, and how little by any known medical means. He therefore directed, with his usual humanity and modesty, that any medicine which he might prescribe, by way of experiment, should not be administered, where the aversion of the patient was great; unless the general health strongly indicated its necessity; well aware, that otherwise, the probable good would not be equal to the certain injury.

There is, however, one remedy, which is very frequently employed at the Retreat, and which appears to have been attended with the happiest effects; and that is the warm bath. In the first years of the Institution, this remedy was not so much employed, as it is at present; for it was natural to pay most attention to such means, as medical writers, professing experience in the treatment of the maladies of the mind, had most strongly recommended: and it is not a little remarkable, that, of the various means proposed for the cure of these disorders few, if any, are less recommended than the warm bath. This remedy, however, has been for several years, and it still is considered, at the Retreat, of greater importance and efficacy, in most cases of melancholia, than all the other medical means which have been employed.

Dr. Willis appears aware of the importance of warm bathing, in cases of insanity, by the answer which he gave to a question upon that subject, from a select Committee of the House of Commons, on the " 9th of March, 1807." This remedy, however, at that time, had been employed for several years with great advantage at the Retreat.

" *Question.* Are you of opinion, that warm and cold baths are necessary for lunatic patients?"

" *Answer.* I think warm baths may be *very useful ;* but, it can seldom happen that a cold bath will be required*."

---

* Vide Report from the Select Committee, appointed to inquire into the state of lunatics. *Haslam's Observations*, p. 336.

That this remedy deserves the attention it receives in this Institution, appears evident by the unusual number of recoveries, in cases of melancholia, to which class the warm bath is chiefly applied. In several cases where the use of this means has been necessarily suspended, the patient has evidently relapsed. No advantage has been found from its use, in case of mania; indeed, it has been thought rather to aggravate the symptoms. The time of the patient's continuance in the bath, and the temperature at which it is used, are gradually increased; the former from twenty minutes to nearly an hour; and the latter, from 85 to 98 degrees.

The cold bath has been frequently tried in a variety of cases, both of melancholia and mania; but the result of the experiments is said to be unfavourable to its general use. In one case, during a paroxysm of high ungovernable mania, immersion of the body, except the head, in the cold bath, for the space of one or two minutes, appeared essentially useful in quieting the patient; but the remedy, in such cases, ought to be applied with great judgment; and its application should always be witnessed by the master, or mistress of the family.

Having shown the result of the experiments made by the respectable physician, who first attended the Retreat officially; it is almost unnecessary to say, that his conclusions have, since, considerably influenced his successors. This, however, has not been entirely the case. Anxious to remove the difficulties that have hitherto attended every attempt, to relieve this most deplorable of human maladies, they have had recourse to various means, suggested either by their own knowledge and ingenuity, or recommended by later writers; but their success has not been such, as to rescue this branch of their profession, from the charge, unjustly exhibited by some against the art of medicine in general, of its being chiefly conjectural.

It must not, however, be supposed, that the office of physician, is considered at the Retreat, of little importance. The physician, from his office, sometimes possesses more influence over the patients' minds, than the other attendants; and in all cases where the mental disease, is attended by any bodily disorder; and more especially when it has supervened any obvious malady, however slight; judicious medical attention, has been found of the greatest advantage. The improvement of one part of the system, has so frequently and regularly kept pace with that of the other, as to leave no doubt of the great importance of attention to the general health of insane patients. The inexplicable sympathy between body and mind, appears to exist, in a morbid degree, in this description of persons; and to them, the remark of Dr. Beddoes, that there is more connexion between a sound mind and a sound body than is generally imagined, is peculiarly applicable. A degree of indigestion, or a fulness of the blood-vessels, which, in others, occasions only a head-ache, or a slight degree of mental inactivity, often produces, in habits where the tendency to insanity is strong, a violent maniacal paroxysm; and has frequently been attended by an accession of the diseased symptoms; or by a relapse when convalescence appeared approaching.

We are, however, far from adopting it as a universal maxim, that maniacal symptoms are aggravated by bodily disorder. On the contrary, several instances have occurred, at the Retreat, of what Dr. Ferrier has termed " conversions;" in which the latter disease has apparently suspended or obliterated the former; and many in which severe bodily indisposition has attended the patient, without any abatement of the maniacal symptoms. These instances by no means lessen the importance of attending to the bodily indications of insane persons; more especially during lucid intervals, or the period of convalescence. From attention to this branch of medical treatment, very great advantage appears to have been derived, at the Retreat.

Topical bleeding has been found eminently useful, where the approach of a paroxysm, was indicated by a determination of blood to the head. In one case particularly, in which the paroxysms had previously been frequent, their return was apparently delayed, for a great length of time, by the judicious use of the scarifying instrument, applied to the shoulders and back of the neck; and on this means of prevention being withheld, a relapse shortly ensued. Hence, we cannot but perceive the importance of insane patients being under the frequent observation of persons of knowledge, judgment, and probity. Hence also an argument arises against very large Institutions, where the number of patients is too great, to come under the proper inspection of the superintendent; and where they are therefore chiefly left to the care and management of keepers, who too frequently possess

I

few of the qualities necessary for their office, unless
we consider as such,

"Limbs of British oak, and nerves of wire."

The difficulty of obtaining sleep for maniacal
patients, and the unpleasant effects frequently produced by the use of opium, are well known to
medical practitioners. It occurred, however, to the
sensible mind of the superintendent, that all animals
in a natural state, repose after a full meal; and,
reasoning by analogy, he was led to imagine, that a
liberal supper would perhaps prove the best anodyne.
He therefore caused a patient, whose violent excitement of mind indisposed him to sleep, to be supplied
freely with meat, or cheese and bread, and good
porter. The effect answered his expectation; and
this mode of obtaining sleep, during maniacal
paroxysms, has since been very frequently and
successfully employed. In cases where the patient
is averse to take food, porter alone has been used
with evident advantage, always avoiding, in all cases,
any degree of intoxication.

Since writing the above, I have been informed, that
a mode somewhat similar, was practised at a private
establishment of some celebrity, in Lancashire. It

was a regular custom in that house, for all the patients to be shut up in their lodging-rooms, for at least an hour after dinner; and it is said, but I am not in possession of particular information on this point, that numerous cures were performed under this treatment. The application, however, of any single means, to all cases, can hardly be judicious.

It has been, and it still is very common, to treat insanity with too little discrimination. Of this practice we have a striking instance in one of our largest public Institutions. I presume not to pry further into the practices of this establishment, than I am enabled to do by the statements of the professional attendants, which have been recently published. The surgeon informs us, that "The curable patients in Bethlem Hospital, are regularly bled about the commencement of June, and the latter end of July*:" and the apothecary to the same Institution tells us; " It has been for many years the practice, to administer to the curable patients, four or five emetics in the spring of the year." He adds, " but on consulting my book of cases, *I have not*

* Crowther on Insanity, page 102.

found that such patients have been particularly
benefited by the use of this remedy *."

It appears that this indiscriminate treatment of
insanity, is not confined to Bethlem Hospital.—Dr.
Pinel, after ridiculing the enormous catalogue of
powders, extracts, juleps, electuaries, draughts, and
epithems, which are recommended in books, as remedies of great virtue, in cases of insanity, says : "What
are we to think of the practice of repeated blood-
letting, *which is so universally the fashion of the present
day*, without attention to the distinctions of the
existing cause, the varieties of sex, or of individual
constitution; and the different species and periods
of the complaint?"

Dr. Arnold,—in the introduction to his Observations
on Insanity, states, that one end he proposes by his
remarks is, to point out " the great variety of those
disorders, which are called by the general appellation
of madness, insanity, or lunacy ; and, to put a stop
to the usual practice of imprudently trusting their
unhappy friends, who have the misfortune to be
afflicted with so various, terrible, and obstinate a

---

* Haslam's Observations on Madness, page 329.

disease, to the common *empirical* practice of *in-discriminate evacuation*, not to mention harsh and cruel treatment, in the hands of any *illiterate pretender !*"

Under the head " Medical Treatment," as practised in the Retreat, some may possibly inquire, what are the means employed in mortifications, arising from cold and confinement ? " a calamity, which," says a writer before alluded to, " frequently happens to the helpless insane, and to bed-ridden patients; as my attendance in a large work-house, in private mad-houses, and Bethlem Hospital, can amply testify *."

Haslam also observes, that the patients in Bethlem Hospital, " are particularly subject to mortifications of the feet; and this fact is so well established from former accidents, that there is an express order of the house, that every patient, under strict confinement, shall have his feet examined every morning and evening in the cold weather, by the keeper, and also have them constantly wrapped in flannel; and those who are permitted to go about, are always

* Crowther, p. 61.

I 3

to be found as near to the fire as they can get, during
the winter season *."

Dr. Pinel also confesses, that " seldom has a whole
year elapsed, during which no fatal accident has
taken place, in the Hospital de Bicêtre, (in France,)
from the action of cold upon the extremities."

Happily, in the Institution I am now describing,
this calamity is hardly known ; and no instance
of mortification has occurred, in which it has been,
in any degree, connected with cold or confinement.   Indeed, the patients are never found to
require such a degree of restraint, as to prevent the
use of considerable exercise, or to render it at all
necessary to keep their feet wrapped in flannel.

It will be proper here to observe, that the experience of the Retreat, fully confirms the opinion of
several respectable modern writers, that maniacs are
by no means exempted from the common effects
of cold ; and it is to be hoped, for the sake of
humanity, that the opposite opinion, alike barbarous
and absurd, will be entirely exploded.   The apothecary

---

* Observations on Madness, p. 84.

to Bethlem Hospital, after stating that the patients are not exempt from the usual effects of severe cold, observes very justly : " From the great degree of insensibility which prevails, in some states of madness, a degree of cold would scarcely be felt by such persons, which would create uneasiness in those of sound mind ; but experience has shown that they suffer equally from severity of weather. When the mind is particularly engaged on any subject, external circumstances affect us less, than when unoccupied Every one must recollect, that in following up a favourite pursuit, his fire has burned out without his being sensible of the alteration of temperature; but when the performance has been finished, or he has become indifferent to it from fatigue, he then becomes sensible to cold, which he had not experienced before."

In considering the medical treatment of the insane, we must not overlook the generally important considerations of diet, air, and exercise. I do not find that many experiments have been made, at the Retreat, upon the subject of diet. The usual bill of fare for the patients on the charity, is such as I imagine will be considered adapted to persons in common health. It is as follows :

Breakfast—Milk and bread, or milk porridge.

Dinner—Pudding and animal food five days in the week; fruit pudding, and broth or soup, two days.

In the afternoon, the men have bread and beer, the women tea or coffee.

Supper—Generally the same as breakfast, or bread, cheese, and beer.

The superior patients have no particular diet, but live in all respects as the superintendents.

Those practitioners who are disposed to recommend a very spare diet, in nearly all cases of insanity, will probably be startled at this account of the mode of living at the Retreat; and those more discriminating persons, of whose curative means, the antiphlogistic, or, in plain English, the reducing system, forms so essential a part of treatment, wherever " irritation or violence exists," may be disposed to consider our diet as more liberal than judicious. So many instances, however, have occurred of complete recovery, after a full trial, previously to admission, had been ineffectually given to diet and medicaments of a reducing nature; that the managers of this establishment, feel no inclination to alter their present plan. I am assured by our physician, who, in his own practice, has had extensive opportunity of observation, that he has seen very few cases, in which a low diet has produced a good effect. On the contrary, " those maniacs who refused their food, have had generally the strongest and most durable paroxysms, and their subsequent depression has been the most deplorable."

Case 74, affords very striking evidence in favour of a liberal, nourishing diet, even where great " irritation or violence exists." The patient was described as a furious, dangerous lunatic; and the reducing system had been fully tried upon him, with an aggravation of his complaint. The opposite mode was then pursued; and his appetite, from being long famished, was almost voracious for many days. It gradually lessened, till it arrived at the common standard. He took no medicine; and under the treatment he met with, his irritation of mind gradually subsided, and his recovery was very rapid and complete.

I will, however, venture to express my doubts, whether the Retreat diet be sufficiently discrimina-tive. In most, if not in all cases of insanity, the animal spirits appear to be either excited or depressed beyond their proper bounds. Knowing, as we do, the effect of food upon ourselves, is it not rational to suppose, that an opposite or different diet, will, in some cases, be required in these opposite states of mind? Pursuing the same track of analogy, which proved so successful in the discovery of the means of obtaining sleep, may we not be led to infer the diet, which is best adapted to some, at least, of the different classes of insanity? The effect of diet upon our dispositions and habits, has been generally admitted. Eschylus makes the king of Pelasgia say to the herald who threatened him with war,

> " You shall be met by men whose lively blood,
> " Dull draughts of barley wine have never clogg'd."

Every one will probably have observed, that after eating a hearty dinner, he is indisposed either to mental or bodily exertion; nor can the different degrees of this indolent feeling which prevail, according to the quantity or nature of the food employed, have escaped notice.

The difference in the French and English character, has been in part attributed to the different mode of living in regard to diet? In France, melancholy is said to be a stranger; whilst with us, and certainly we have long had more political right to be merry, melancholy, and hence suicide, is proverbially common *. Some writers are, however, of opinion, that this fatal propensity, does not, in any degree, arise from the cause we have just mentioned. Dr. Beddoes says, " there are few countries in Europe, of which the inhabitants do not consume as much animal food as the corresponding classes of the English." Be this as it may, the importance of attention to diet, appears to me to derive sufficient

---

* " I cannot," says a medical observer, " by any means persuade myself that the excess of the English in animal food, has any thing to do with the frequency of self-murder, in their otherwise fortunate island. For in Bavaria, Austria, and other provinces of the German empire, far more butchers' meat is served up than in England, and far more eaten. Yet with us, suicide is a far more unfrequent occurrence. That we, in fact, eat a greater quantity of meat than the English, I was convinced of, by the entertainments at which I was present in London. And I still recollect with pleasure, an incident to this purpose that took place at Coventry. At an inn in that city, my fellow-travellers and myself bespoke all the articles in the bill of fare. They were about six, and we were obliged to repeat our order to the waiter three several times, and at last were interrogated by the landlady herself, whether we had in earnest ordered all that meat. So simple is English fare.——*Salzburg Med. Chirurg. Zeetung.* 1798, *l.* 170."

Beddoes' Essay on Consump. page 111.

support from the general effect of different kinds of
food on our mental feelings.

After apologizing to the reader for this speculative
digression, I return to the more useful detail of practical results. The absurd notion respecting the
capacity of maniacs generally to resist the action of
cold, has been already mentioned. The supporters
of this opinion, also generally observe, that insane
persons commonly endure hunger without injury.—
The latter sentiment is no less at variance with the
experience of the Retreat, than the former. Some of
the patients, more especially the melancholics and
convalescents, besides their four usual meals in the
day, require the intermediate refreshment of biscuit,
with a glass of wine or porter ; and attention of this
kind is considered almost essential to the recovery of
many patients.

" General propositions," says Dr. Pinel, " have
been too often advanced in regard to the capacity
of maniacs to bear extreme hunger with impunity.
I have known several, who were voracious to a great
degree, and who languished, even to fainting, from
want, or deficiency of nourishment. It is said of an
asylum at Naples, that a low spare diet is a funda-

mental principle of the Institution. It would be
difficult to trace the origin of so singular a prejudice.
Unhappy experience, which I acquired during
seasons of scarcity, has most thoroughly convinced
me, that insufficiency of food, when it does not
altogether extinguish the vital principle, is not a
little calculated to exasperate and prolong the
disease *."

I would not have dwelt so long upon these mistaken opinions, if they had not furnished a specious
pretext for much practical barbarity; and I am,
therefore, anxious to see them ranked with the mar-
vellous stories of the Phœnix and the Salamander.

Where various means are employed, it is difficult
to say which is the operative one; but, whatever may
be the means used, there is great reason to believe
that a clear dry air, which the situation of the Retreat
affords in an eminent degree, will facilitate their
operation, and be favourable to the recovery of insane
persons. To reason again from analogy; the general
effects of fine air upon the animal spirits, would
induce us to expect especial benefit from it, in cases

* Dr. Davis's translation of " Pinel's Treatise on Insanity," p. 31.

of mental depression; and to pay all due respect to
the physician, who,

> " Gives melancholy up to Nature's care,
> " And sends the patient into purer air."

Several instances have occurred, in which melancholy patients, have been very much improved by
their journey to the Retreat; and it is the decided
opinion of the manager of this Institution, that, in
such cases, close confinement is of all things the most
detrimental.

CHAPTER V.

MORAL TREATMENT.

─────

SECTION I.

INTRODUCTORY OBSERVATIONS.

Importance of Management in a curative point of view——
Power of self-control possessed by Maniacs——The
disorder generally partial, in regard to both the
intellectual powers and affections——Of the malevo-
lent dispositions evinced by Maniacs——Powerful
effect of judicious kindness——Practices of the
Retreat arranged under three heads.

WHATEVER theory we maintain in regard to the remote causes of insanity, we must consider moral treatment, or management, of very high importance.

If we adopt the opinion, that the disease originates in the mind, applications made immediately to it, are obviously the most natural ; and the most likely to be attended with success. If, on the contrary, we conceive that mind is incapable of injury or destruction, and that, in all cases of apparent mental derangement, some bodily disease, though unseen and unknown, really exists, we shall still readily admit, from the reciprocal action of the two parts of our system upon each other, that the greatest attention is necessary, to whatever is calculated to affect the mind.

In the present imperfect state of our knowledge, of the very interesting branch of the healing art, which relates to the cure of insanity ; and unable as we generally are to ascertain its true seat in the complicated labyrinths of our frame, the judicious physician is very frequently obliged to apply his means, chiefly to the alleviation and suppression of symptoms.

Experience, however, has happily shown, in the Institution whose practices we are attempting to describe, that much may be done towards the cure and alleviation of insanity, by judicious modes of management, and moral treatment. The super-intendent, who is also the apothecary of the Retreat, after more than fifteen years experience, fully unites with the intelligent Dr. Pinel, in his comparative esti-mate of moral and medical means. The doctor thus

expresses himself : " Attaching, as I do, little importance to pharmaceutic preparations; and, all-sufficiency,
in curable cases, to physical and moral regimen, I
intend not to devote many of my pages, to the exclusive consideration of drugs and medicaments."

It is a matter of no small difficulty, to convey
more than the general principles which influence the
conduct of those, who have the management of the
insane. It is unhappily, in great measure true, that
" the address which is acquired by experience, and
constant intercourse with maniacs, cannot be communicated : it may be learned; but it must perish
with its possessor *." It appears, however, to me,
that a free detail of different modes of management,
can hardly fail to increase our stock of correct general
principles, on this important subject.

Insane persons generally possess a degree of control over their wayward propensities. Their intellectual, active, and moral powers, are usually rather
perverted than obliterated; and it happens, not un-

---

* Observations on Madness, by John Haslam, p. 277, 2d edition ;
from which all the quotations in this work are taken. The Retreat,
at an early period, derived advantage from the first edition of these
Observations.

K

frequently, that one faculty only is affected. The disorder is sometimes still more partial, and can only be detected by erroneous views, on one particular subject. On all others, the mind appears to retain its wonted correctness.

The same *partial* perversion, is found to obtain in this disease with regard to the affections. Though it frequently happens, that indifference or disgust towards the tenderest connexions, is an early and distressing symptom of insanity; when,

> ——————— " forgotten quite,
> " All former scenes of dear delight,
> " Connubial love, parental joy ;
> " No sympathies like these his soul employ ;"

yet the existence of the benevolent affections, is often strongly evidenced, by the patient's attachment to those who have the immediate care of them, and who treat them with judgment and humanity. The apothecary to Bethlem Hospital says *, " I can truly declare, that by gentleness of manner, and kindness of treatment, I have seldom failed to obtain the confidence, and conciliate the esteem, of insane persons; and have succeeded by these means in procuring from

---

* Observations, p. 293.

them respect and obedience." The superintendents of
the Retreat give precisely the same evidence ; and I
firmly believe, that a large majority of the instances, in
which the malevolent dispositions are peculiarly apparent, and are considered as characterizing the disorder,
may readily be traced to secondary causes ; arising
from the peculiar circumstances of the patient, or
from the mode of management.

A patient confined at home, feels naturally a
degree of resentment, when those whom he has been
accustomed to command, refuse to obey his orders,
or attempt to restrain him. We may also, I conceive, in part, attribute to similar secondary causes,
that apparent absence of the social affections, and
that sad indifference to the accustomed sources of
domestic pleasure, of which we have just been
speaking. The unhappy maniac is frequently un-
conscious of his own disease. He is unable to
account for the change in the conduct of his wife,
his children, and his surrounding friends. They
appear to him cruel, disobedient, and ungrateful.
His disease aggravates their conduct in his view, and
leads him to numerous unfounded suspicions. Hence,
the estrangement of his affections may frequently be
the natural consequence, of either the proper and

K 2

necessary, or of the mistaken conduct of his friends towards him.

In such cases, the judicious kindness of others appears generally to excite the gratitude and affection of the patient. Even in those deplorable instances where the ingenious humanity of the superintendent fails to conciliate, and the jaundice-like disease, changes the very aspect of nature, and represents all mankind as the leagued enemies of the patient, the existence of the social affections, has often been strikingly evidenced, by attachment to some of the inferior animals.

There are, undoubtedly, cases in which the disorder is chiefly marked by a mischievous malevolent disposition; but of these, very few have occurred at the Retreat. There have, however, been many patients, in whom these dispositions have been occasionally conspicuous, or easily excited by improper treatment.

The outline of the character of the insane, which we have now exhibited, must be considered as confined to two states of the disease, mania and melancholia. It frequently happens, however, that a greater or less degree of imbecility, succeeds the more violent excitement of the mind ; and a sufficient number of cases of this description have occurred, to warrant me in asserting, that even in these hopeless instances of mental alienation *, considerable

---

* I adopt this term from an opinion, that the *aliéné.* of the French, conveys a more just idea of this disorder, than those expressions which imply, in any degree, the " abolition of the thinking faculty." The following case, related to me by a medical friend, will serve to show that even in idiocy, the mind may be rather suppressed than destroyed. A young woman, who was employed as a domestic servant, by the father of the relater, when he was a boy, became insane, and at length sunk into a state of perfect idiocy. In this condition she remained for many years, when she was attacked by a typhus fever ; and my friend, having then practised some time, attended her. He was surprised to observe, as the fever advanced, a development of the mental powers. During that period of the fever, when others were delirious, this patient was entirely rational. She recognized, in the face of her medical attendant, the son of her old master, whom she had known so many years before ; and she related many circumstances respecting his family, and others, which had happened to herself in her earlier days. But, alas ! it was only the gleam of reason ; as the fever abated, clouds again enveloped the mind ; she sunk into her former deplorable state, and remained in it until her death, which happened a few years afterwards. I leave to the metaphysical reader, further speculation on this, certainly, very curious case.

K 3

warmth of affection is frequently evinced ; and that patients of this class may, in general, be easily amused and pleased.

If the preceding sketch is correct, it would not, I apprehend, be difficult to infer theoretically, the general principles of moral treatment and management ; but I have happily little occasion for theory, since my province is to relate, not only what ought to be done, but also what, in most instances, is actually performed.

The moral treatment of the insane, seems to divide itself into three parts ; and under these, the practices of the Retreat may be arranged. We shall therefore inquire,

I. By what means the power of the patient to control the disorder, is strengthened and assisted.

II. What modes of coercion are employed, when restraint is absolutely necessary.

III. By what means the general comfort of the insane is promoted.

SECTION II.

OF THE MEANS OF ASSISTING THE PATIENT TO CONTROL HIMSELF.

*Power of self-restraint strongly evidenced at the
Retreat——Motives for its exertion——Conclusion
drawn hence respecting the excitement of Fear——
Of the degree in which Fear may be usefully excited——Of the excitement of furious Mania by
improper treatment; and of the efficacy of persuasion and kind treatment towards inducing self-
restraint——Argument in favour of the terrific
system. Of the attendants' behaviour to lunatics
on first acquaintance——Analogy between the judicious treatment of children and insane persons——Of
the manner of speaking to Maniacs——Of reasoning
with the Patient on the subject of his hallucination——
Of the conversation adapted to melancholics——
Beneficial effects of exercise and variety of object
upon this class, illustrated by an affecting case——
Advantage of regular labour in some cases——
Desire of esteem a powerful principle towards
inducing self-restraint——Other means of cultiva-
ting it——The aid of Religion in promoting self-
restraint——Hints to the attendants on the Insane.*

WE have already observed, that most insane
persons, have a considerable degree of self command;
and that the employment and cultivation of this

K 4

remaining power, is found to be attended with the most salutary effects. Though many cannot be made sensible of the irrationality of their conduct or opinions; yet they are generally aware of those particulars, for which the world considers them proper objects of confinement. Thus it frequently happens, in the Institution we are describing, that a patient, on his first introduction, will conceal all marks of mental aberration. Instances have occurred, in which the struggle has been so successful, that persons, who, on undoubted authority, have been declared to be unmanageable at home; and to have shown very striking marks of insanity ; have not, for a very considerable time, exhibited sufficient symptoms of the disorder, to enable the physician to declare them, *non compos mentis.* Doubtless the idea that their early liberation, for which most are anxious, and their treatment during their confinement, will depend, in great measure, on their conduct, has a tendency to produce this salutary restraint, upon their wayward propensities.— Hence, also, the idea seems to have arisen, that madness, in all its forms, is capable of entire control, by a sufficient excitement of the principle of fear. This speculative opinion, though every day's experience decidedly contradicts it, is the best apology which can be made for the barbarous practices that have often prevailed in the treatment of the insane.

The principle of fear, which is rarely decreased by insanity, is considered as of great importance in the management of the patients. But it is not allowed to be excited, beyond that degree which naturally arises from the necessary regulations of the family. Neither chains nor corporal punishments are tolerated, on any pretext, in this establishment. The patients, therefore, cannot be threatened with these severities; yet, in all houses established for the reception of the insane, the general comfort of the patients ought to be considered; and those who are violent, require to be separated from the more tranquil, and to be prevented, by some means, from offensive conduct, towards their fellow-sufferers. Hence, the patients are arranged into classes, as much as may be, according to the degree in which they approach to rational or orderly conduct.

They quickly perceive, or if not, they are informed on the first occasion, that their treatment depends, in great measure, upon their conduct. Coercion thus flowing as a sort of necessary consequence, and being executed in a manner which marks the reluctance of the attendant, it seldom exasperates the violence of the patient, or produces that feverish and sometimes furious irritability, in which the maniacal character is completely developed; and under which all power of self-control is utterly lost.

There cannot be a doubt that the principle of fear, in the human mind, when moderately and judiciously excited, as it is by the operation of just and equal laws, has a salutary effect upon society. It is a principle also of great use in the education of children, whose imperfect knowledge and judgment, occasion them to be less influenced by other motives. But where fear is too much excited, and where it becomes the chief motive of action, it certainly tends to contract the understanding, to weaken the benevolent affections, and to debase the mind. As the poet of Liberty has well sung,

———————————————" All constraint,

" Except what wisdom lays on evil man,

" Is evil; hurts the faculties, impedes

" Their progress in the road of science, blinds

" The eye-sight of discovery; and begets, '

" In those that suffer it, a sordid mind,

" Bestial, a meagre intellect, unfit

" To be the tenant of man's noble form."

COWPER'S TASK, BOOK V.

It is therefore wise to excite, as much as possible, the operation of superior motives; and fear ought only to be induced, when a *necessary* object cannot otherwise be obtained. If this is the true scale of estimating the degree in which this principle is, in general, to be employed, it is found, at the Retreat, equally applicable to the insane.

That the continual or frequent excitement of the sensations of fear, should " bid Melancholy cease to mourn," is an idea too obviously absurd in theory, to require the refutation of experience. There has, however, unhappily been too much experience on this subject; and hence we may perhaps, in great degree, explain, why melancholy has been consider-ed so much less susceptible of cure than mania. To the mild system of treatment adopted at the Retreat, I have no doubt we may partly attribute, the happy recovery of so large a proportion of melancholy patients.

Is then the violent excitement of the principle of fear, better adapted to enable the maniac to control his wanderings, and to suppress his emotions? Is it not well known, that the passions of many maniacs, are extremely irritable? and, when once excited,

are not all moral means to subdue them, as in-
effectual as the attempt would be to quench, by
artifical means, the fires of Etna ?

If it be true, that oppression makes a *wise* man
mad, is it to be supposed that stripes, and insults,
and injuries, for which the receiver knows no cause,
are calculated to make a *madman* wise? or would
they not exasperate his disease, and excite his resentment ? May we not hence most clearly perceive,
why furious mania, is almost a stranger in the
Retreat ? why all the patients wear clothes, and are
generally induced to adopt orderly habits ?

The superintendent of this Institution is fully of
opinion, that a state of furious mania, is very often
excited by the mode of management. Of this
opinion, a striking illustration occurred in this
Institution, some years ago. A patient, of rather
a vindictive and self-important character, who had
previously conducted himself with tolerable propriety, one day, climbed up against a window,
which overlooked the court where he was confined,
and amused himself by contemplating the interior
of the room. An attendant, who had not been long
in office, perceiving his situation, ran hastily

towards him, and, without preamble, drew him to
the ground. The patient was highly incensed; a
scuffle immediately ensued, in which he succeeded
in throwing his antagonist; and had not the loud
vociferations of this attendant alarmed the family, it is
probable that he would have paid for his rash conduct,
by the loss of his life. The furious state of the
patient's mind did not continue long ; but, after this
circumstance, he was more vindictive and violent.

In some instances, the superintendent has known
furious mania temporarily induced, by the privations
necessary on a relapse, after a considerable lucid
interval, during which the patient had enjoyed many
privileges, that were incompatible with his disordered
state. Here we may suggest the expediency, where
it is possible, of employing such of the attendants to
control the patient during his paroxyms, as had little
intercourse with him in his lucid interval. Instances
of furious mania have been, however, very rare ; but
a considerable number of patients have been admitted,
who were reported to be so furiously insane, as to
require constant coercion.

The evidence of attendants, who have been employed, previously to the admission of patients into

the Retreat, is not considered a sufficient reason for any extraordinary restraint; and cases have occurred, in which persuasion and kind treatment, have superseded the necessity of any coercive means.

Some years ago a man, about thirty-four years of age, of almost Herculean size and figure, was brought to the house. He had been afflicted several times before; and so constantly, during the present attack, had he been kept chained, that his clothes were contrived to be taken off and put on by means of strings, without removing his manacles. They were however taken off, when he entered the Retreat, and he was ushered into the apartment, where the superintendents were supping. He was calm; his attention appeared to be arrested by his new situation. He was desired to join in the repast, during which he behaved with tolerable propriety. After it was concluded, the superintendent conducted him to his apartment, and told him the circumstances on which his treatment would depend; that it was his anxious wish to make every inhabitant in the house, as comfortable as possible; and that he sincerely hoped the patient's conduct would render it unnecessary for him to have recourse to coercion. The maniac was sensible of the kindness of his treatment. He promised to restrain himself, and he so completely succeeded, that, during his stay, no coercive means were ever employed towards him. This case affords a striking example of the efficacy of mild treatment. The patient was frequently very vociferous, and threatened his attendants, who in their defence were very desirous of restraining him by the jacket. The superintendent on these occasions, went to his apartment; and though the first sight of him seemed rather to increase the patient's irritation, yet after sitting some time quietly beside him, the violent excitement subsided, and he would listen with attention to the persuasions and arguments of his friendly visiter. After such conversations, the patient was generally better for some days or a week; and in about four months he was discharged perfectly recovered.

Can it be doubted, that, in this case, the disease had been greatly exasperated by the mode of management? or that the subsequent kind treatment, had a great tendency to promote his recovery?

It may probably be urged, and I am very well aware of it, that there is a considerable class of patients, whose eccentricities may, in great measure, be controlled; and who may be kept in subjection and apparent orderly habits, by the strong excitement of the principle of fear. They may be made to obey their keepers, with the greatest promptitude; to rise, to sit, to stand, to walk, or run at their pleasure; though only expressed by a look. Such an obedience, and even the appearance of affection, we not unfrequently see in the poor animals who are exhibited to gratify our curiosity in natural history; but, who can avoid reflecting, in observing such spectacles, that the readiness with which the savage tiger obeys his master, is the result of treatment, at which humanity would shudder; and shall we propose by such means,

     " To calm the tumult of the breast,
     " Which madness has too long possest ;
     " To chase away the fiend Despair,
     " To clear the brow of gloomy Care ;
     " Bid pensive Melancholy cease to mourn,
       " Calm Reason reassume her seat;
     " Each intellectual power return?"

If those who are friendly to what may be termed the terrific system of management, could prove, that, notwithstanding it may fix for life, the misery of a large majority of the melancholics; and drive many of the more irritable maniacs to fury or desperation; yet that it is still, in its operation upon a large scale, adapted to promote the cure of insanity, they would have some apology for its discriminate adoption. If, on the contrary, a statement of the proportion of cures in the Retreat, shall sufficiently prove the superior efficacy of mild means, would not those, who are adopting an opposite line of treatment, do well to reflect on the awful responsibility which attaches to their conduct ? Let us all constantly remember, that there is a Being, to whose eye darkness is light; who sees the inmost recesses of the dungeon, and who has declared: " For the sighing of the poor, and the crying of the needy, I will arise."

From the view we have now taken of the propriety of exciting fear, as a means of promoting the cure of insanity, by enabling the patient to control himself, it will, perhaps, be almost superfluous to state as our opinion, that the idea, which has too generally, obtained, of its being necessary to commence an acquaintance with lunatics, by an exhibition of strength, or an appearance of austerity, is utterly erroneous. The sentiment appears allied to that cruel system, probably dictated by indolence and timidity, which has so long prevailed, and unhappily still prevails, in many receptacles for the insane.

L

There is much analogy between the judicious treatment of children, and that of insane persons. Locke has observed, that " the great secret of education, lies in finding the way to keep the child's spirit easy, active, and free; and yet, at the same time, to restrain him from many things he has a mind to, and to draw him to things which are uneasy to him." It is highly desirable that the attendants on lunatics should possess this influence over their minds; but it will never be obtained by austerity and rigour; nor will assumed consequence, and airs of self-importance, be generally more successful.

Much familiarity with maniacal patients, on their first introduction to a new situation, is not thought, in general, to be advisable. It might, in some instances, have a tendency to lessen that authority, which is, occasionally, necessary for the attendant to exert. There may also be a few cases in which a distant, and somewhat important manner, may be assumed with advantage; but, generally speaking, even with regard to the more violent and vociferous maniacs, a very different mode is found successful; and they are best approached with soft and mild persuasion. The superintendent assures me, that in these cases, he has found it peculiarly necessary to speak to the patient in a kind, and somewhat low tone of voice. So true are the maxims of antiquity,

" A soft answer turneth away wrath."—SOLOMON.

——————————" Soft speech

" Is to distemper'd wrath, medicinal."—ESCHYLUS.

It must, however, be understood, that the persuasion which is extended to the patients, is confined to those points which affect their liberty or comfort. No advantage has been found to arise from reasoning with them, on their particular hallucinations. One of the distinguishing marks of insanity, is a fixed false conception, which occasions an almost total incapacity of conviction. The attempt, therefore, to refute their notions, generally irritates them, and rivets the false perception more strongly on their minds. There have been a few instances, in which, by some striking evidence, the maniac has been driven from his favourite absurdity ; but it has uniformly been succeeded by another equally irrational.

In regard to melancholics, conversation on the subject of their despondency, is found to be highly injudicious. The very opposite method is pursued. Every means is taken to seduce the mind from its

favourite but unhappy musings, by bodily exercise,
walks, conversation, reading, and other innocent
recreations. The good effect of exercise, and of
variety of object, has been very striking in several
instances at this Institution. Some years ago, a
patient much afflicted with melancholic and hypochondriacal symptoms, was admitted by his own
request. He had walked from home, a distance of
200 miles, in company with a friend ; and on his
arrival, found much less inclination to converse on
the absurd and melancholy views of his own state,
than he had previously felt*.

----

* Though this patient was much less disposed to converse upon
the subject, his hypochondriacal ideas remained, as the following
description of himself, taken nearly verbatim from his own mouth,
will prove: " I have no soul; I have neither heart, liver, nor lungs ;
nor any thing at all in my body, nor a drop of blood in my veins. My
bones are all burnt to a cinder : I have no brain ; and my head is
sometimes as hard as iron, and sometimes as soft as a pudding." A
fellow patient, also an hypochondriac, amused himself in versifying
this affectingly ludicrous description in the following lines:

> A miracle, my friends, come view,
> A man, admit his own words true,
>   Who lives without a soul ;
> Nor liver, lungs, nor heart has he,
> Yet, sometimes, can as cheerful be
>   As if he had the whole.

This patient was by trade a gardener, and the
superintendent immediately perceived, from the
effect of this journey, the propriety of keeping him
employed. He led him into the garden, and con-
versed with him on the subject of horticulture ; and
soon found that the patient possessed very superior
knowledge of pruning, and of the other departments
of his art. He proposed several improvements in
the management of the garden, which were adopted,
and the gardener was desired to furnish him with full
employment. He soon, however, showed a reluctance
to regular exertion, and a considerable disposition to
wandering, which had been one of the previous

His head (take his own words along)
Now hard as iron, yet ere long
    Is soft as any jelly ;
All burnt his sinews, and his lungs ;
Of his complaints, not fifty tongues
    Could find enough to tell ye.

Yet he who paints his likeness here,
Has just as much himself to fear,
    He's wrong from top to toe ;
Ah friends ! pray help us, if you can,
And make us each again a man,
    That we from hence may go.

L 3

features of his complaint. The gardener was repeatedly charged to encourage him in labour, and
to prevent his leaving the premises. But, unhappily,
the superior abilities of the patient, had excited a
jealousy in the gardener's mind, which made him
dislike his assistance; and it may therefore be presumed, that he obeyed his instructions very im-
perfectly.

The poor man rambled several times from the
grounds of the Institution; which, in his state of
mind, excited considerable anxiety in the family.
Of course it became necessary to confine him more
within doors. He frequently, however, walked out ;
and the superintendent took many opportunities
to attend him into the fields or garden, and to engage
him for a time in steady manual labour. As his
disorder had increased, it became difficult to induce
him to exert himself; but even in this state, when he
had been some time employed, he seemed to forget his
distressful sensations and ideas, and would converse
on general topics with great good sense.

In this truly pitiable case, the superintendent
several times tried the efficacy of long walks,
where the greatest variety and attraction of circum-

stances were presented; but neither these, nor the
conversation which he introduced, were able to draw
the patient so effectually from the " moods of his
own mind," as regular persevering labour in the
garden. It is not improbable, however, that the
superior manner in which the patient was able to
execute his work, produced a degree of self-com-
placency which had a salutary effect; and that, had
his education enlarged his curiosity, and encouraged
a taste and observation respecting the objects of
nature and art, he might have derived much greater
advantage, as many patients obviously do, from
variety of conversation and scenery.

The circumstances of this patient did not allow
him a separate attendant, and the engagements of the
superintendent were too numerous and important,
to permit him to devote to this case the time and
attention which it seemed to require. He has
frequently expressed to me, the strong feelings of
regret, which were excited in his mind, by the
unsuccessful treatment of this patient; the case
certainly points out the great importance of exercise
and labour, in the moral treatment of insanity;
more especially in cases of melancholy.

This patient, after remaining several years in the house, died of an acute inflammation of the bowels. His situation for a considerable time previously to his death, was most deplorable, and has often reminded me of the affecting description, which our great poet gives of the state of our first father, after his expulsion from the happy seat of primeval innocence:

———————————————————————" On the ground,
" Outstretch'd he lay, on the cold ground, and oft
" Curs'd his creation, death as oft accus'd
" Of tardy execution."

The female patients in the Retreat, are employed, as much as possible, in sewing, knitting, or domestic affairs; and several of the convalescents assist the attendants. Of all the modes by which the patients may be induced to restrain themselves, regular employment is perhaps the most generally efficacious; and those kinds of employment are doubtless to be preferred, both on a moral and physical account, which are accompanied by considerable bodily action; that are most agreeable to the patient, and which are most opposite to the illusions of his disease.

In an early part of this chapter, it is stated, that the patients are considered capable of rational and honourable inducement; and though we allowed *fear* a considerable place in the production of that restraint, which the patient generally exerts on his entrance into a new situation; yet the *desire of esteem* is considered, at the Retreat, as operating, in general, still more powerfully. This principle in the human mind, which doubtless influences, in a great degree, though often secretly, our general manners; and which operates with peculiar force on our intro-duction into a new circle of acquaintance, is found to have great influence, even over the conduct of the insane. Though it has obviously not been sufficiently powerful, to enable them entirely to resist the strong irregular tendencies of their disease; yet when properly cultivated, it leads many to struggle to conceal and overcome their morbid propensities; and, at least, materially assists them in confining their deviations, within such bounds, as do not make them obnoxious to the family.

This struggle is highly beneficial to the patient, by strengthening his mind, and conducing to a salutary habit of self-restraint; an object which experience points out as of the greatest importance, in the cure of insanity, by moral means.

That fear is not the only motive, which operates in producing *self-restraint* in the minds of maniacs, is evident from its being often exercised in the presence of strangers, who are merely passing through the house ; and which, I presume, can only be accounted for, from that desire of esteem, which has been stated to be a powerful motive to conduct.

It is probably from encouraging the action of this principle, that so much advantage has been found in this Institution, from treating the patient as much in the manner of a rational being, as the state of his mind will possibly allow. The superintendent is particularly attentive to this point, in his conversation with the patients. He introduces such topics as he knows will most interest them ; and which, at the same time, allows them to display their knowledge to the greatest advantage. If the patient is an agriculturist, he asks him questions relative to his art ; and frequently consults him upon any occasion in which his knowledge may be useful. I have heard one of the worst patients in the house, who,

previously to his indisposition, had been a considerable grazier, give very sensible directions for the
treatment of a diseased cow.

These considerations are undoubtedly very material,
as they regard the comfort of insane persons; but
they are of far greater importance, as they relate
to the cure of the disorder. The patient feeling
himself of some consequence, is induced to support
it by the exertion of his reason, and by restraining
those dispositions, which, if indulged, would lessen
the respectful treatment he receives; or lower his
character in the eyes of his companions and attendants.

They who are unacquainted with the character
of insane persons, are very apt to converse with
them in a childish, or, which is worse, in a domineering
manner; and hence it has been frequently remarked
by the patients at the Retreat, that a stranger
who has visited them, seemed to imagine they were
children.

The natural tendency of such treatment is, to
degrade the mind of the patient, and to make him
indifferent to those moral feelings, which, under

judicious direction and encouragement, are found capable, in no small degree, to strengthen the power of self-restraint ; and which render the resort to coercion, in many cases, unnecessary. Even when it is absolutely requisite to employ coercion, if the patient promises to control himself on its removal, great confidence is generally placed upon his word. I have known patients, such is their sense of honour and moral obligation, under this kind of engagement, hold, for a long time, a successful struggle with the violent propensities of their disorder ; and such attempts ought to be sedulously encouraged by the attendant.

Hitherto we have chiefly considered those modes of inducing the patient to control his disordered propensities, which arise from an application to the general powers of the mind ; but considerable advantage may certainly be derived, in this part of moral management, from an acquaintance with the previous habits, manners, and prejudices of the individual. Nor must we forget to call to our aid, in endeavouring to promote self-restraint, the mild but powerful influence of the precepts of our holy religion. Where these have been strongly imbued in early life, they become little less than principles of our nature ; and their restraining power is frequently felt, even under the delirious excitement of insanity. To encourage the influence of religious principles over the mind of the insane, is considered of great consequence, as a means of cure. For this purpose, as well as for others still more important, it is certainly right to promote in the patient, an attention to his accustomed modes of paying homage to his Maker.

Many patients attend the religious meetings of the Society, held in the city; and most of them are assembled, on a first day afternoon, at which time the superintendent reads to them several chapters in the Bible. A profound silence generally ensues; during which, as well as at the time of reading, it is very gratifying to observe their orderly conduct, and the degree in which those, who are much disposed to action, restrain their different propensities.

In pursuing these desirable objects, let not the inexperienced, but judicious attendant, expect too immediate effects from his endeavours, or be disheartened by occasional disappointment. Let him bear in mind, what the great Lord Bacon has admirably said, that "It is order, pursuit, sequence, and interchange of application, which is mighty in

nature; which, although it require more exact knowledge in prescribing, and more precise obedience in
observing, yet is recompensed with the magnitude of
effects." *

I am sensible that what is here stated, is but an
imperfect view of the principles and modes, by which
self-restraint is induced at the Retreat. To particularize all the principles of the mind, which may
be usefully excited in promoting this salutary object,
would be an enumeration of our intellectual powers
and affections. I will only further observe upon this
head, by way of general summary, that the attendant
on the insane, ought sedulously to endeavour to gain
their confidence and esteem; to arrest their attention,
and fix it on objects opposite to their illusions; to
call into action, as much as possible, every remaining
power and principle of the mind; and to remember
that, in the wreck of the intellect, the affections not
unfrequently survive.

----

* Works, 8vo edition, vol. i. p. 125.

SECTION III.

OF THE MODES OF COERCION.

*General view of the nature of coercion used at the Retreat
——Mode of coercing violent Maniacs, and Melancholics disposed to self-destruction——Experience of
the Retreat in regard to indulging the ebullition of
violent Maniacs——Causes of the too general use of
coercion——Of the degree of force to be employed
when coercion is necessary——Modes of coercing the
less violent——Precautionary measures——Necessity
of experience to teach the best modes of restraint.*

WITH regard to the second point, the necessity of
coercion, I have no hesitation in saying, that it will
diminish or increase, as the moral treatment of the
patient is more or less judicious. We cannot, however, anticipate that the most enlightened and ingenious humanity, will ever be able entirely to
supersede the necessity of personal restraint.

Coercion is considered, as the ingenious author of
" Observations on Madness" says it should be,
" only as a protecting and salutary restraint." The
mode of it ought to be subject to the consideration

of its effect on the mind of the insane. Some means of coercion have obviously a greater tendency than others, to irritate or degrade the feelings. Hence, the use of chains has never been permitted in the Retreat. In the most violent states of mania, as the author just quoted observes, " the patient should be kept alone, in a dark* and quiet room ; so that he may not be affected by the stimulus of light or sound ; such abstraction more readily disposing to sleep. As in this violent state, there is a strong propensity to associate ideas, it is particularly important to prevent the accession of such, as might be transmitted through the medium of the senses†." The patients of this class, who are not disposed to injure themselves, are merely confined by the strait-waistcoat; and left to walk about the room, or lie down on the bed, at pleasure. But in those desperate cases of melancholy, attended with tedium vitæ, in which there is a strong determination to self-destruction, it becomes necessary to confine the patient, during the night, in a recumbent posture. For this purpose, the super-

---

* Our superintendent prefers a gloomy, to an entirely dark apartment.

† The necessity for this mode of treatment is very rare at the Retreat.

intendent has invented a very simple apparatus; which answers all the purposes of security; and allows the patient to turn and otherwise change his posture in bed *.

It has been suggested, that in cases of high mania, the violent excitement would be best reduced, by indulging it in the greatest practicable degree. The experience of the Retreat, leads to an opposite conclusion; viz. that such a degree of restraint as would not be materially painful, in a state of calmness, has a tendency to abate the paroxysm. The association

---

* This apparatus consists of a strong, linen, girth web, three inches and a half broad, and five feet and a half long. At each end is a leather strap one foot long, one inch and a half broad, and a quarter of an inch thick; with a buckle fastened at the joining of the web and strap. At eighteen inches from the upper end of the web, a piece of the same materials, fourteen inches long, placed transversely, is strongly sewed to it. Each end of this cross piece is provided with two straps one inch and a quarter broad, and about three-sixteenths of an inch thick. One of these straps is five inches long, provided with a buckle, and a piece of leather inside the buckle to prevent it from hurting the arm. The other strap is fifteen inches long, with holes to buckle to the former; and both are strongly sewed together with the web between them. At twenty-one inches from the lower end of the web, are fixed transversely, two leather straps of the same strength as those last described. Both are

M

between mental and bodily action, and the degree in
which the latter is well known to excite the former,
sufficiently illustrate the cause of this fact.

Except in the case of violent mania, which is far
from being a frequent occurrence at the Retreat,
coercion, when requisite, is considered as a necessary
evil; that is, it is thought abstractedly to have a tendency to retard the cure, by opposing the influence
of the moral remedies employed. It is therefore used
very sparingly; and the superintendent has often
assured me, that he would rather run some risk, than

----

strongly sewed together on the web, by the middle; one extending
six inches beyond the web on each side, and provided at each end
with a buckle and a guard, as before-mentioned: the other is two
feet long, with perforations at each end. When in use, the main
strap passes longitudinally over the lower bed-clothes, and is fastened
to the head and feet of the bedstead, by a proper staple fixed in the
centre of each, and is buckled tight. The patient is placed upon it; the
cross web at the upper end is placed under the shoulders, and each
pair of straps at the ends of this transverse piece, encloses one arm;
but is not buckled so tight as to hurt the patient. The lower pair of
straps each enclose one thigh, just above the knee, in like manner.

In many cases of violent excitement, this is found sufficient; but
where the patient is ingenious, or disposed to self-injury, the addition
of the strait-waistcoat is needful.

have recourse to restraint, where it was not absolutely necessary; except in those cases where it was likely to have a salutary moral tendency.

I feel no small satisfaction in stating upon the authority of the superintendents, that during the last year, in which the number of patients has generally been sixty-four, there has not been occasion to seclude, on an average, two patients at one time. I am also able to state, that although it is occasionally necessary to restrain by the waistcoat, straps, or other means, several patients at one time; yet that the average number so restrained does not exceed four, including those who are secluded.

The safety of those who attend upon the Insane, is certainly an object of great importance; but it is worthy of inquiry whether it may not be attained, without materially interfering with another object,— the recovery of the patient. It may also deserve inquiry, whether the extensive practice of coercion, which obtains in some Institutions, does not arise from erroneous views of the character of insane persons; from indifference to their comfort; or from having rendered coercion necessary by previous unkind treatment.

M 2

The power of judicious kindness over this unhappy class of society, is much greater than is generally imagined. It is perhaps not too much to apply to kind treatment, the words of our great poet,

———————————————— " She can unlock,
" The clasping charm, and thaw the numbing spell."—MILTON.

In no instances has this power been more strikingly displayed; or exerted, with more beneficial effects, than in those deplorable cases in which the patient refuses to take food. The kind persuasions and ingenious arts of the superintendents, have been singularly successful in overcoming this distressing symptom ; and very few instances now occur in which it is necessary to employ violent means for supplying the patient with food.

Some patients who refuse to partake of the family meals, are induced to eat by being taken into the larder, and there allowed to help themselves. Some are found willing to eat when food is left with them in their rooms, or when they can obtain it unobserved by their attendants. Others, whose determination is stronger, are frequently induced, by repeated persuasion, to take a small quantity of nutritious liquid ; and it is equally true in these, as in general cases, that every breach of resolution weakens the power and disposition to resistance.

Sometimes, however, persuasion seems to strengthen the unhappy determination. In one of these cases, the attendants were completely wearied with their endeavours; and on removing the food, one of them took a piece of the meat which had been repeatedly offered to the patient, and threw it under the fire-grate; at the same time, exclaiming, that she should not have it. The poor creature, who seemed governed by the rule of contraries, immediately rushed from her seat, seized the meat from the ashes, and devoured it. For a short time, she was induced to eat, by the attendants availing themselves of this contrary disposition, but it was soon rendered unnecessary, by the removal of this unhappy feature of the disorder.

There are, it must be confessed, some cases in which ingenious arts, and kind persuasions, prove alike unsuccessful; and it becomes necessary to supply the patient by force with a sufficient quantity of food, to support life. This is, perhaps, the most painful duty, which the attendant has to perform. It is usually done at the Retreat in the following

M 3

manner: The patient is placed in a rocking chair,
which of course allows the height and position of the
head to be varied, as circumstances may require.
The most difficult part of the business is, if I may
use the expression, to unlock the mouth. For this
purpose, the superintendent, after trying a variety of
instruments, generally employs the handle of a small
door lock key, and having pressed it between the
teeth, he turns it round by the other end, and
thereby raises the mouth at his pleasure. Another
attendant then introduces the food, which is in a
liquid state, and contained in a strong spoon. I
am very glad to be able to say, that there is seldom
occasion for the frequent repetition of this operation;
and also that it has not, in a single instance, been
the occasion of any injury to the patient*. The

---

* " It is a painful recollection, to recur to the number of interesting
females I have seen, who, after having suffered a temporary dis-
arrangement, and undergone the brutal operation of spouting, in
private receptacles for the insane, have been restored to their
friends without a front tooth in either jaw. Unfortunately the task
of forcing patients to take food or medicines, is consigned to the
rude hand of an ignorant and unfeeling servant. It should always
be performed by the master or mistress of the mad-house, whose
reputations ought to be responsible for the personal integrity of the
unhappy beings committed to their care."

Haslam's Observations on Madness, note, page 137.

teeth of few persons meet with perfect regularity, and this circumstance greatly facilitates the insertion of the instrument which keeps them asunder. It is found necessary to convey the point of the spoon, half way over the tongue; for when the liquid is not conveyed into the throat, it is frequently ejected.

The attendants at the Retreat, feel themselves in no danger of injury from the patients, who are unconfined; many of whom, previously to their admission, have been accustomed to much severity. No instance has occurred of any serious injury being done by a patient, to any of the attendants; and at no period has there been manifested a general spirit of dissatisfaction, or a tendency to revolt.

The **common** attendants, are not allowed to apply any extraordinary coercion to the patients, by way of punishment, or to change, in any degree, the usual mode of treatment, without the permission of the superintendents. This limitation to their power is of the utmost importance, as it obliges them to seek the good opinion of the patient, and to endeavour to govern rather by the influence of esteem than of severity.

M 4

When it is deemed necessary to apply the strait-waistcoat, or any other mode of coercion, to a violent patient, such an ample force is employed, as precludes the idea of resistance from entering the patient's mind; and hence, irritation, or additional excitement, is generally, in a great degree, prevented.

Where such force cannot be obtained, and the case is urgent, courage and confidence will generally overcome the violence of the patient ; for the opinion appears to be well founded, that maniacs are seldom truly courageous. The superintendent was one day walking in a field adjacent to the house, in company with a patient, who was apt to be vindictive on very slight occasions. An exciting circumstance occurred. The maniac retired a few paces, and seized a large stone, which he immediately held up, as in the act of throwing at his companion. The superintendent, in no degree ruffled, fixed his eye * upon the patient, and in a resolute tone of voice, at the same time advancing, commanded him to

---

* My worthy friend does not, however, lay any claim to

" Those strange powers, which lie

" Within the magic circle of the eye."

lay down the stone. As he approached, the hand of the lunatic gradually sunk from its threatening position, and permitted the stone to drop to the ground. He then submitted to be quietly led to his apartment *.

Some of the more irritable patients, who are neither vindictive nor violent, require, occasionally, a degree of restraint, to prevent them from injuring their companions, or destroying their clothes. This class is chiefly found among those whose intellects are weakened. These are sometimes restrained by straps which pass round the ankles, and prevent the patient from kicking ; or are confined, when neces-sary, by arm-straps, fixed to a belt which encircles the waist. These straps allow the patient to use his hands sufficiently to feed himself; and are abundantly less uneasy than the strait-waistcoat. Some of the female patients of this description, have the straps made of green morocco leather, and they will sometimes even view their shackles as ornaments. The reader will find an account of several precautionary means in the third chapter. To those, I here wish to add, that the patients, who take their meals in the

* See another circumstance respecting this patient, related page 13.

galleries, or day-rooms, are not allowed the use of knives and forks *. Their meat is divided into small pieces by the attendant, and they eat it with a spoon. It is also the business of the attendant to take the patient's clothes out of the lodging-room, and examine the pockets every night.

I conceive it useless to enter into more minute details of the modes of coercion and restraint, since experience alone can fully teach the best means of exercising them; and the attendant who possesses a good understanding, and has taken a just view of the character of the insane, will soon perceive for himself, the necessary degree, time, and mode of coercion, which those who are placed under his care require. But they who have had an opportunity of observation, and they only, can conceive the difficulty of entirely subduing the vindictive feelings, which the inconsistent, but often half rational, conduct of the patient, frequently excites in the minds of the inferior attendants.

------

* The superintendent hopes to be able to contrive a knife and fork that may be entrusted to most of the patients with safety; as it would be much more agreeable to many of them, than eating all their food with a spoon.

It is therefore an object of the highest importance, to infuse into the minds of these persons, just sentiments, with regard to the poor objects placed under their care ; to impress upon them, that " coercion is only to be considered as a protecting and salutary restraint ;" and to remind them, that the patient is really under the influence of a disease, which deprives him of responsibility ; and frequently leads him into expressions and conduct the most opposite to his character and natural dispositions :

> " Bound in Necessity's iron chain,
>   Reluctant Nature strives in vain ;
>   Impure, unholy thoughts succeed,
>   And dark'ning o'er his bosom roll ;
>   Whilst madness prompts the ruthless deed,
>   Tyrant of the misguided soul."

But even this view of the subject is not exempt from danger; if the attendant does not sufficiently consider the degree in which the patient may be influenced by moral and rational inducements. These contradictory features in their character, frequently render it exceedingly difficult to insure the proper treatment of deranged persons. To consider them at the same

time both as brothers, and as mere automata; to ap-
plaud all they do right; and pity, without censuring,
whatever they do wrong, requires such a habit of
philosophical reflection, and Christian charity, as is
certainly difficult to attain.

SECTION IV.

OF THE MEANS OF PROMOTING THE GENERAL COMFORT OF THE INSANE.

*Importance of promoting comfort as it regards cure——
Various means of promoting it at the Retreat——
Utility of rational society to convalescent Patients——
The different kinds of amusing employments adapted
to different classes of Patients——On the introduction
of books to the Insane——Importance of arresting
their attention——Case——Difficulty of devising
suitable employments.*

IN considering our first division of this subject, viz.
the modes by which self-restraint may be induced,
we have anticipated many of the means by which
the comfort of this unhappy class of our fellow
beings is promoted; indeed we might, without im-
propriety, have included all these means under our
former division; since whatever tends to promote
the happiness of the patient, is found to increase his
desire to restrain himself, by exciting the wish not
to forfeit his enjoyments; and lessening the irritation
of mind, which too frequently accompanies mental
derangement.

The comfort of the patients is therefore considered of the highest importance, in a curative point of view The study of the superintendents to promote it with all the assiduity of parental, but judicious attention, has been, in numerous instances, rewarded by an almost filial attachment. In their conversation with the patients, they adapt themselves to their particular weaknesses; but, at the same time, endeavour to draw them insensibly from the sorrow, or the error, which marks the disease.

The female superintendent, who possesses an uncommon share of benevolent activity, and who has the chief management of the female patients, as well as of the domestic department, occasionally gives a general invitation to the patients, to a tea-party. All who attend, dress in their best clothes, and vie with each other in politeness and propriety. The best fare is provided, and the visiters are treated with all the attention of strangers. The evening generally passes in the greatest harmony and enjoyment. It rarely happens that any unpleasant circumstance occurs; the patients control, in a wonderful degree, their different propensities; and the scene is at once curious, and affectingly gratifying.

Some of the patients occasionally pay visits to the friends in the city; and female visiters are appointed every month, by the Committee, to pay visits to those of their own sex; to converse with them, and to propose to the superintendents, or the Committee, any improvements which may occur to them. The visiters sometimes take tea with the patients, who are much gratified with the attention of their friends, and mostly behave with propriety.

It will be necessary here to mention, that the visits of former intimate friends, have frequently been attended with disadvantage to the patients; except when convalescence had so far advanced, as to afford a prospect of a speedy return to the bosom of society. It is, however, very certain, that as soon as reason begins to return, the conversation of judicious, indifferent persons, greatly increases the comfort; and is considered almost essential to the recovery of many patients. On this account, the convalescents of every class, are frequently introduced into the society of the rational parts of the family. They are also permitted to sit up till the usual time for the family to retire to rest, and are allowed as much liberty as their state of mind will admit*.

* The patients usually rise at seven in summer, and eight in winter; and the common time of going to bed is eight o'clock.

Those who have had the opportunity of observing the restoration of reason, will be aware, that she does not, in general, at once, resume her lost empire over the mind. Her approach resembles rather the gradual influx of the tide; she seems to struggle to advance, but again and again is compelled to recede. During this contest, the judicious attendant, may prove the most valuable ally of reason; and render to her the most essential assistance, in the recovery of her lawful throne:

In some cases, however, the cloud which envelopes the mind is suddenly dispersed, and the patient seems to awake at once as out of a dream. In others the progress of recovery is gradual and uniform:

——————————————" Lucid order dawns;
" And as from chaos old the jarring seeds
" Of Nature, at the voice divine, repair'd
" Each to its place, 'till rosy earth unveil'd
" Her fragrant bosom, and the joyful sun
" Sprung up the blue serene ; by swift **degrees**
" Thus disentangled," [reason entire]
" Emerges."
The Pleasures of Imagination, Book III. l. 396.

As indolence has a natural tendency to weaken the mind, and to induce ennui and discontent, every kind of rational and innocent employment is encouraged. Those who are not engaged in any useful occupation, are allowed to read, write, draw, play at ball, chess, drafts, &c.*

The attendant will soon perceive what kind of employment or amusement, is best adapted to the different patients under his care. He will observe that those of the most active and exciting kind, will be best adapted to the melancholy class, where they can be induced to engage in them ; and that the more sedentary employments, are generally preferable for the maniacal class. No strict rule, however, can properly be laid down on this subject ; and the inclination of the patient may generally be indulged, except the employment he desires obviously tends to foster his disease. The means of writing, are, on this account, sometimes obliged to be withheld from the patient, as it would only produce continual essays on his peculiar notions ; and serve to fix his errors more completely in his mind. Such patients are, however, *occasionally* indulged, as it is found to give

---

* It is, perhaps, almost unnecessary to state, that playing for money, or gaming of any kind, is not allowed.

N

them temporary satisfaction; and to make them more easily led into suitable engagements*.

---

* This indulgence in the means of writing, frequently leads to curious effusions, both in prose and poetry. The following specimen of the latter, will probably interest the reader. He will be surprised to learn, that the patient, at the time of its composition, laboured under a very considerable degree of active mania. This is not the only instance in which we have been reminded of the lines of the poet,

" Great wit to madness, sure, is near allied,
" And thin partitions do their bounds divide."

ADDRESS TO MELANCHOLY.

SPIRIT of darkness! from yon lonely shade
  Where fade the virgin roses of the spring;
Spirit of darkness, hear thy fav'rite maid
  To Sorrow's harp her wildest anthem sing.

Ah! how has Love despoil'd my earliest bloom,
  And flung my charms as to the wintry wind;
Ah! how has Love hung o'er thy trophied tomb,
  The spoils of genius, and the wreck of mind.

High rides the moon the silent heavens along;
  Thick fall the dews of midnight o'er the ground;
Soft steals the Lover, when the morning song
  Of waken'd warblers thro' the woods resound.

Then I, with thee, my solemn vigils keep,
  And at thine altar take my lonely stand;
Again my lyre, unstrung, I sadly sweep,
  While Love leads up the dance, with harp in hand.

High

MORAL TREATMENT. 183

There certainly requires considerable care in the selection of books for the use of the insane. The works of imagination are generally, for obvious reasons, to be avoided; and such as are in any degree connected with the peculiar notions of the patient, are decidedly objectionable. The various branches of the mathematics and natural science, furnish the most useful class of subjects on which to employ the minds of the insane; and they should, as much as possible, be induced to pursue one subject steadily. Any branch of knowledge with which

---

High o'er the woodlands Hope's gay meteors shone,
　　And thronging thousands bless'd the ardent ray ;
I turn'd, but found Despair on his wild roam,
　　And with the demon bent my hither-way.

Soft o'er the vales she blew her bugle horn,
　　Oh! where MARIA, whither dost thou stray ?
Return, thou false maid, to th' echoing sound,
　　I flew, nor heeded the sweet syren's lay.

Hail, Melancholy! to yon lonely towers
　　I turn, and hail thy time-worn turrets mine,
Where flourish fair the night-shade's deadly flowers,
　　And dark and blue, the wasting tapers shine.

There, O my EDWIN ! does thy spirit greet
　　In fancy's maze thy lov'd and wandering maid;
Soft thro' the bower thy shade MARIA meets,
　　And leads thee onward thro' the myrtle glade.

O, come

the patient has been previously acquainted, may be resumed with greater ease; and his disposition to pursue it will be encouraged by the competency which he is able to exhibit.

I met with a striking instance, of the advantage of attention to this point, some years ago. It was related to me by a person of great respectability, who was himself the subject of the case. He stated, that a few years before that time, his mind had been greatly depressed without any apparent cause. The

O, come with me, and hear the song of eve,
    Far sweeter, far, than the loud shout of morn;
List to the pantings of the whispering breeze,
    Dwell on past woes, or sorrows yet unborn.

We have a tale; and song may charm these shades,
    Which cannot rouse to life MARIA's mind,
Where Sorrow's captives hail thy once lov'd maid,
    To joy a stranger, and to grief resign'd.

EDWIN, farewell! go, take my last adieu,
    Ah! could my bursting bosom tell thee more,
Here, parted here, from love, from life, and you,
    I pour my song as on a foreign shore.

But stay, rash youth, the sun has climb'd on high,
    The night is past, the shadows all are gone,
For lost MARIA breathe the eternal sigh,
    And waft thy sorrows to the gales of morn.

most dismal thoughts continually haunted his mind,
and he found the greatest difficulty, in confining his
attention, for the shortest time, to one subject. He
felt entirely indifferent to his business and his family ;
and, of course, he neglected them. It was with
great difficulty he was induced to take sufficient food
to support life. His body became emaciated, and
his mind more and more enfeebled.

In this state, as he was one day musing upon his
miserable condition, he perceived, by the faint glim-
merings of remaining reason, the still worse state to
which he must be reduced, if he continued to indulge
his gloomy reflections and habits. Alarmed with
the prospect of the future, he resolved to exert the
power which he still possessed to control his unhappy dispositions, and to regain the habit of attention. For this purpose, he determined, immediately
to apply himself to mathematics, with which he had
been well acquainted in his youth, and also to adopt
a more liberal regimen.

The first attempt to go through the easiest pro-
blem, cost him indescribable labour and pain. But
he persisted in the endeavour ; the difficulty of fixing
his attention gradually lessened ; he overcame his

tendency to abstinence; and very shortly recovered the use of his faculties and his former temper of mind.

Perhaps few persons, in the situation which I have described, would have had the courage to form such resolutions; and still fewer, the fortitude to perform them. The case, however, certainly points out what may possibly be done; and how important it is, in a curative point of view, to encourage the patient in steady mental pursuit.

The managers of this Institution, are far from imagining that they have arrived at a state of perfection in the moral treatment of insanity. If they have made any considerable approaches towards it, their progress has only served to convince them how much more may probably be effected, and to fill them with regret, that so little ingenuity has hitherto been exerted to increase the comforts of insane persons. There is no doubt, that if the same exertions were used for this purpose, as are frequently employed to amuse the vain, the frivolous, and the idle, many more gleams of comfort would be shed over the unhappy existence of lunatics; and the proportion of cures would be still materially increased.

What a reflection upon human nature, that the greatest calamity to which it is incident, should have been frequently aggravated by those who had the power, and whose duty it was to employ means of mitigation. Hence, we may derive a practical comment on the observation of the wise Montesquieu, which every one interested in establishments for the insane ought constantly to remember: "Cest une experience éternelle, que tout homme qui a du pouvoir est porté, à en abuser; il va jusqu' à ce qu'il trouve des limites. Qui le diroit! La vertu même a besoin des limites *.

L'Esprit des Loix, Liv. II. Cap. IV.

---

* Experience continually demonstrates, that men who possess power, are prone to abuse it: they are apt to go to the utmost limits. May it not be said, that the most virtuous require to be limited?

N 4

CHAPTER VI.

STATEMENT OF CASES AND REMARKS.

TABLE OF CASES

Admitted into the Retreat, from its opening in the year 1796, to the end of the year 1811; exhibiting the result, or present state of each.

———

☞ In the following table, M. signifies married; S. single; W. widower, or widow; O. C. old case; R. C. recent case; Mo. month; Man. mania; Mel. melancholia; H. M. hypochondriac melancholy; Dem. dementia, or maniacal imbecility; 96 D. 04 D. &c, died 1796, 1804, &c. ; Recov. recovered; Imp. improved; M. I. much improved; V. M. I. very much improved.

———

Number.	Age of Males.	Age of Fem.	Single or Mar.	Old or Recent.	Description of Disorder.	When admitted. Mo.	Discharged, Deceased, &c. Mo.	In what state.
1		65	M	O C	Man.	6, 1796	3, 1808	Imp.
2		60	S	O C	Man.	6,	Remains	
3	26		S	O C	Man.	6,	12, 96 D.	Mel.
4		50	M	R C	Mel.	7,	1, 1810	Recov.
5	26		S	O C	Man.	8,	6, 04 D.	

———

APPARENT CAUSE, &c.

No. 3. Disappointment of the affections.

No. 5. Supervened epilepsy.

———

* The design of exhibiting the state of the patients to a later period than that of their admission, is, obviously, to allow time to see the effect of their being placed in the Institution. It may not, however, be improper to add, that from the end of the year 1811, about fifteen months, fourteen patients have been admitted; and that in the three months since the end of 1812, four patients have recovered, and no death has occurred.

Number.	Age of Males.	Age of Fem.	Single or Mar.	Old or Recent.	Description of Disorder.	When admitted. Mo.	Discharged, Deceased, &c. Mo.	In what state.
6		25	S	O C	Man.	7, 1796	Remains	
7		50	S	O C	Man.	8,	Remains	
8	45		M	O C	Man.	8,	Remains	
9		26	S	R C	Mel.	8,	4, 97 D.	Imp.
10		52	S	O C	Man.	9,	Remains	
11		52	S	O C	H. M.	9,	8, 1800	Recov.
12	30		S	O C	Dem.	9,	Remains	
13	39		M	O C	Mel.	11,	5, 1800	Recov.
14		55	M	O C	Mel.	12,	11, 1798	Recov.
15	32		S	O C	Mel.	12,	Remains	
16	45		S	O C	Man.	2, 1797	12, 1798	M. I.
17	74		W	O C	H. M.	4,	10, 1804	M. I.
18		54	S	O C	Man.	5,	1, 1811	Imp.
19		72	S	O C	Man.	7,	Remains	
20		47	S	O C	Man.	7,	7, 05 D.	Imp.
21	45		S	R C	Man.	1, 1798	1, 1799	M. I.
22	24		S	O C	Man.	2,	7, 09 D.	
23		20	S	R C	Man.	3,	6, 1798	Recov.
24		45	S	O C	Man.	3,	7, 1806	Recov.
25		45	S	O C	Man.	6,	3,	Recov.

APPARENT CAUSE, &c.

No. 10. Succeeded a disappointment of the affections

No. 13. Constitutional.

No. 15. Constitutional.

No. 16. Succeeded disappointment in business.

No. 17. Constitutional.

No. 19. Succeeded disappointment of affections.

No. 21. Constitutional.

No. 23. Succeeded family misfortunes.

No. 25. Succeeded disappointment of affections.

Number.	Age of Males.	Age of Fem.	Single or Mar.	Old or Recent.	Description of Disorder.	When admitted.	Discharged Deceas'd, &c.	In what state.
						Mo.	*Mo.*	
26	32		M	R C	Man.	6, 1798	6, 98 *D.*	
27	24		S	O C	Mel.	7,	Remains	
28		24	S	O C	Man.	7,	Remains	
29		36	M	R C	Man.	8,	11, 1798	M. I.
30	50		W	O C	Man.	7,	9, 02 *D.*	
31	60		W	O C	Man.	9,	1, 00 *D.*	Imp.
32		22	S	R C	Mel.	10,	Remains	M. I.
33	43		S	O C	Man.	11,	Remains	
34	46		M	O C	Mel.	11,	6, 00 *D.*	
35	54		S	O C	Mel.	12,	3, 05 *D.*	
36		38	S	R C	Mel.	12,	6, 1799	Recov.
37		26	S	O C	Man.	2, 1799	9, 00 *D.*	Imp.
38	50		S	O C	Man.	3,	5, 01 *D.*	Imp.
39	48		M	O C	H. M.	5,	6, 09 *D.*	
40	60		S	O C	Dem.	5,	4, 00 *D.*	
41		24	S	O C	Mel.	6,	10, 1803	Recov.
42		20	S	R C	Mel.	8,	10,	Recov.

APPARENT CAUSE, &c.

No. 27. Succeeded disappointment of affections.

No. 28. Contusion of the skull.—Habit predisposed to the disorder.

No. 30. Succeeded the death of his wife.

No. 32. Disorder hereditary—Excited by over-attention to her mother in her last illness, and the subsequent sorrow.

No. 33. Succeeded disappointment of affections.

No. 34. Succeeded disappointment in business.

No. 37. Epilepsy.

No. 38. Hereditary.

No. 42. Hereditary—Succeeded means used to check violent perspiration, which supervened a pleuritic attack.

Number.	Age of Male.	Age of Fem.	Single or Mar.	Old or Recent.	Description of Disorder.	When admitted.	Discharged, Deceased, &c.	In what state.
						Mo.	Mo.	
43		40	S	O C	Mel.	9, 1799	Remains	Dem.
44		19	S	R C	Man.	9,	11, 1801	Recov.
45		30	S	O C	Man.	9,	Remains	
46		36	S	O C	Man.	3, 1800	7, 08 D.	Dem.
47		27	M	R C	Man.	3,	6, 1800	Recov.
48		22	S	R C	Man.	4,	12,	Recov.
49	60		M	R C	Mel.	4,	12,	Recov.
50	17		S	R C	Man.	6,	11, 1801	Recov.
51	68		M	O C	H. M.	6,	Remains	
52		22	S	O C	Mel.	6,	Remains	
53		22	S	O C	Man.	7,	Remains	Dem.
54		25	S	O C	Man.	7,	Remains	
55		37	S	R C	Man.	8,	11, 1812	Recov.
56	27		S	R C	Man.	10,	4, 1802	Recov.
57	34		S	R C	Mel.	10,	5, 1801	Recov.
58		40	S	O C	Man.	12,	4, 1811	Recov.

APPARENT CAUSE, &c.

No. 45. Hereditary.

No. 46. Supervened epilepsy.

No. 47. Succeeded the failure of her husband in business.

No. 48. Succeeded the failure of her father in business.

No. 49. Very melancholy temperament.

No. 53. Succeeded disappointment of the affections.

No. 54. Naturally of weak intellect.

No. 55. Constitutional—Succeeded Hysteria, brought on by the death of a friend.

No. 56. Constitutional—Appeared to be excited by irregular conduct.

No. 57. Succeeded disappointment of affections.

No. 58. Constitutional.

Number.	Age of Males	Age of Fem.	Single or Mar.	Old or Recent.	Discription of Disorder.	When admitted.	Discharged, Deceased, &c.	In what state.
						Mo.	Mo.	
59		25	S	O C	Man.	12, 1800	Remains	
60	50		M	O C	Man.	2, 1801	5, 1802	Recov.
61		69	M	R C	Mel.	3,	5, 06 D.	
62	20		S	O C	Dem.	5,	Remains	
63	66		W	R C	Mel.	8,	3, 1802	Recov.
64		21	S	R C	Mel.	10,	3,	Recov.
65		25	S	R C	Mel.	10,	7,	Recov.
66		30	S	R C	Man.	11,	Remains	
67		22	S	R C	Man.	12,	5, 1808	Recov.
68		28	S	R C	Mel.	3, 1802	9, 1802	Recov.
69		35	S	R C	Man.	3,	Remains	
70		52	M	R C	Mel.	5,	9, 1806	M. I.
71	50		S	O C	Man.	7,	8,	Recov.
72		45	M	O C	Mel.	7,	6, 1803	Recov.

APPARENT CAUSE, &c.

No. 59. Very ricketty in childhood—Forehead peculiarly narrow.

No. 60. Constitutional.

No. 61. Succeeded the failure of her husband in business.

No. 62. Constitutional.

No. 63. Succeeded embarrassment of his affairs. Second attack.

No. 64. Disappointment of the affections.

No. 65. Succeeded the death of her father.

No. 66. Constitutional—Accelerated by a fright.

No. 67. Constitutional.

No. 68. Constitutional.

No. 70. The supposed loss of her husband, who was shipwrecked, but saved.

No. 72. Supervened parturition.

Number	Age of Males.	Age of Fem.	Single or Mar.	Old or Recent.	Description of Disorder	When admitted.	Discharged, Deceased, &c.	In what state.
						Mo.	Mo.	
73		22	S	R C	Man.	7, 1802	4, 1803	Recov.
74	34		S	R C	Man.	8,	12, 1802	Recov.
75		60	S	O C	Man.	9,	Remains	
76		28	S	R C	Mel.	11,	6, 1803	Recov.
77		31	S	O C	Mel.	11,	8, 1809	Recov.
78	38		S	O C	Mel.	11,	4, 05 D.	Dem.
79	56		S	O C	Man.	3, 1803	Remains	Imp.
80		38	S	R C	Mel.	5,	5, 1804	Recov.
81	49		M	R C	Mel.	5,	10, 03 D.	
82	28		S	R C	Mel.	6,	4, 1804	Recov.
83	60		M	R C	Man.	10,	7,	Recov.
84	43		W	O C	Man.	12,	Remains	
85		69	W	O C	*	6, 1804	Remains	Imp.

APPARENT CAUSE, &c.

No. 73. The warm bath appeared useful in this case, which has rarely happened in cases of mania.

No. 74. Intemperance—Had been deranged several times before.

No. 75. Attributed to a disappointment of the affections, and being reduced in circumstances.

No. 76. Constitutional.

No. 77. Constitutional—Cessation of copious perspiration of the head.

No. 78. General debility of body and mind.

No. 80. Constitutional.

No. 81. Over-attention to business.

No. 82. Constitutional—The disorder first marked by religious anxiety.

No. 83. Succeeded fever.

No. 84. Constitutional.

---

* Mania and Melancholia intermitting.

Number.	Age of Males.	Age of Fem.	Single or Mar.	Old or Recent.	Description of Disorder.	When admitted.	Discharged, Deceased, &c.	In what state.
						Mo.	Mo.	
86	34		S	O C	Man.	6, 1804	4, 1806	Recov.
87	58		M	R C	Mel.	7,	Remains	Imp.
88		52	M	O C	Man.	7,	10, 1804	M. I.
89	60		S	O C	Man.	10,	Remains	
90		28	S	R C	Mel.	1, 1805	8, 1805	Recov.
91	54		M	O C	Man.	2,	12,	M. I.
92		63	S	O C	Man.	4,	Remains	
93		39	W	R C	Mel.	5,	9, 1806	Recov.
94		44	S	R C	Man.	5,	11,	Recov.
95		18	S	O C	Man.	5,	Remains	Dem.
96	39		S	O C	Man.	7,	Remains	Imp.

APPARENT CAUSE, &c.

No. 86. Succeeded the imprudent use of mercury.

No. 87. Constitutional.

No. 88. First appearance of the disorder marked by trifling, ludicrous religious scruples.

No. 89. Attended with violent head-aches.

No. 90. Constitutional, excited by misfortune and over-exertion.

No. 91. Attributed to the imprudent use of mercury.

No. 93. Constitutional—Opium pill taken in ale always successful in obtaining sleep.

No. 94. Constitutional.

No. 95. No assignable cause.

No. 96. Constitutional. *

---

* This patient, from motives of humanity, had been confined at home twenty years. It had been deemed necessary to keep him mostly chained, and he was generally naked. The only confinement to which he has been subjected at the Retreat, is arm-straps, and these are now seldom requisite. He has been induced to wear clothes, and adopt general orderly habits.

Number.	Age of Males.	Age of Fem.	Single or Mar.	Old or Recent.	Description of Disorder.	When admitted.	Discharged, Deceased, &c.	In what state.
						Mo.		
97		40	S	O C	Man.	7, 1805	Remains	
98		65	S	O C	Mel.	8,	4, 06 D.	
99		55	M	O C	Mel.	9,	2, 1807	Recov.
100		19	S	R C	Man.	9,	8, 1806	Recov.
101	50		M	O C	Man.	12,	Remains	
102	54		S	O C	Man.	1, 1806	2, 11 D.	
103	23		S	O C	Man.	1,	8, 06 D.	Mel.
104	50		S	R C	Mel.	4,	6, 06 D.	
105	52		M	O C	Man.	6,	11, 1806	Imp.
106		59	W	O C	Man.	6,	9, 1811	Imp.
107		64	W	O C	Mel.	7,	9,	Imp.
108	40		S	O C	Man.	7,	Remains	
109		34	S	O C	Man.	12,	Remains	
110	60		M	O C	Man.	12,	11, 1810	Imp.
111	30		W	R C	Mel.	1, 1807	5, 1807	Recov.
112	60		M	O C	Man.	2,	12, 1812	Recov.

APPARENT CAUSE, &c.

No. 99. Constitutional.

No. 100. Succeeded great anxiety of mind.

No. 103. Constitutional, connected with bodily disease.

No. 104. Naturally of a weak capacity.

No. 105. Constitutional—Excited by interest on political subjects, and occasional inebriety.

No. 107. Excited by loss of a son and other afflictions.

No. 108. Connected with the breaking off a matrimonial acquaintance

No. 109. Constitutional.

No. 110. Had been previously confined many years.

No. 111. Constitutional—Excited by the death of his wife.

No. 112. No apparent cause.

O

Number.	Age of Males.	Age of Fem.	Single or Mar.	Old or Recent.	Description of Disorder.	When admitted.	Discharg'd, Deceased, &c.	In what state.
						Mo.		
113	55		S	O C	Man.	4, 1807	Remains	Imp. *
114	25		S	R C	Man.	7,	10, 1808	Recov.
115		24	S	R C	Man.	7,	10,	Recov.
116	23		S	R C	Man.	9,	4,	Recov.
117		57	M	R C	Man.	10,	10, 07 D.	
118		73	S	O C	Dem.	10,	1, 1808	†
119		43	S	R C	‡	1, 1808	Remains	Dem.
120	21		S	O C	Man.	2,	Remains	Dem.
121	27		S	O C	Man.	4,	Remains	

APPARENT CAUSE, &c.

No. 113. Constitutional.

No. 117. Connected with apoplexy.

No. 119. Constitutional.

No. 120. Occasioned by violent fear. §

No. 121. Constitutional.

---

* This case is almost an exact copy of No. 96. The poor man had nearly lost the use of his limbs, and, for a considerable time after his admission, required to be led about like an infant. He now walks without assistance, requires no coercion, and evidently enjoys the change in his situation. On one of his friends visiting him at the Retreat, and inquiring of him what he called the place, he replied, with great earnestness, "Eden, Eden, Eden."

† Not a suitable object.

‡ Dementia, with occasional fits of mania.

§ This young man appears to have been naturally of a timorous disposition, and the family in which he was an apprentice, most inhumanly amused themselves in exciting dreadful apprehensions in his mind. One day, the servant maid, dressed herself in men's clothes, and, armed with a pistol, entered the room in which he was alone. Pointing it at his head, she pretended to shoot him. The

pistol,

Number.	Age of Males.	Age of Fem.	Single or Mar.	Old or Recent.	Description of Disorder.	When admitted.	Discharged, Deceased, &c.	In what state.
						Mo.	Mo.	
122		46	W	R C	*	4, 1808	7, 1808	Recov.
						7, 1811	12, 1812	Recov.
123		21	S	R C	Man.	5, 1808	Remains	Imp.
124	44		S	O C	Mel.	6,	7, 12 D	Man.
125		36	S	R C	Mel.	6,	Remains	Man.
126		38	M	R C	Mel.	8,	11, 08 D	
127		50	S	R C	Mel.	8, 1808	4, 1810	Recov.
						6, 1810	9, 1812	Recov.
128		23	S	O C	Man.	8, 1808	3, 1809	Recov.
129	75		M	O C	Mel.	9,	12, 1808	M. I.
130		60	W	O C	Mel.	10,	Remains	Imp.
131		35	M	R C	Mel.	10,	12, 1809	Recov.

APPARENT CAUSE, &c.

No. 122. Constitutional.

No. 123. Constitutional.

No. 124. Constitutional.

No. 125. Constitutional.

No. 126. Connected with apoplexy.

No. 127. Constitutional.

No. 128. Constitutional

No. 129. Constitutional.

No. 130. Excited by family troubles.

No. 131. Constitutional.—Induced by an unhappy marriage.

---

pistol, of course, was not loaded, but its effects were sufficiently injurious. The poor object of this brutish sport, no longer possessed the command of his reason. He became extremely violent, and, after remaining at home some years, was re-moved to the Retreat; where he remains in a state of hopeless imbecility ! Surely, some punishment should await this intellectual murder !

* Mania, with occasional depression of spirits.

O 2

Number.	Age of Males.	Age of Fem.	Single or Mar.	Old or Recent.	Description of Disorder.	When admitted.	Discharged, Deceased, &c.	In what state.
						Mo.	Mo.	
132		33	S	R C	Mel.	1, 1809	9, 1810	Recov.
133	15		S	O C	Man.	3,	8,	V. M. I.
134	50		M	O C	Dem.	6,	9, 09, *D*	
135	68		W	R C	Mel.	7,	4, 1812	V. M. I.
136	21		S	R C	*	8,	2, 1810	Recov.
137		23	S	R C	Mel.	1, 1810	6,	Recov.
138	23		S	R C	Man.	8,	4, 1811	Recov.
139		50	S	O C	Man.	7,	Remains	
140	40		S	R C	Man.	2, 1811	Remains	
141		34	S	O C	Man.	3,	9, 1812	Recov.
142		25	S	R C	Man.	3,	6, 1811	Recov.
143	28		S	R C	Mel.	3,	Remains	
144	40		S	O C	†	4,	2, 1812	Imp.
						4, 1812	Remains	

APPARENT CAUSE, &c.

No. 132. Constitutional.

No. 134. Injury of the skull.

No. 135. Constitutional.—Had been in the same state before.

No. 136. Disappointment.

No. 137. Constitutional.

No. 138. Constitutional.

No. 139. Constitutional.

No. 140. Constitutional.—Perplexing circumstances in business.

No. 141. Constitutional.—Induced by fright.

No. 142. Constitutional.—Succeeded low fever.

No. 143. Constitutional.—Disappointment in the affections.

No. 144. Constitutional.

---

* Mania and Melancholia intermitting.

† Mania and Melancholia alternately.

Number.	Age of Males.	Age of Fem.	Single or Mar.	Old or Recent.	Description of Disorder.	When admitted.	Discharged, Deceased, &c.	In what state.
						Mo.	Mo.	
145	40		M	R C	Man.	6, 1811	4, 1812	Recov.
146		25	S	R C	Man.	8,	Remains	
147		49	S	O C	Man.	8,	Remains	
148	60		S	O C	Man.	9,	Remains	Imp.
149		30	S	O C	Dem.	12,	9, 1812	*

APPARENT CAUSE, &c.

No. 145. No assignable cause.

No. 146. No cause assigned.

No. 147. Had been previously confined in several houses.

No. 148. Constitutional.

No. 149. Constitutional.

* Not a suitable object.

The preceding statements are given, to enable the reader to judge of the efficacy of the modes of treatment, practised in the Retreat.

It appears, that, from the opening of this Institution, in the year 1796, to the end of the year 1811, one hundred and forty-nine patients have been admitted. Of this number, only sixty-one have been recent cases. Thirty-one of these patients have laboured under mania ; of whom,

2 have died,

6 remain in the house,

21 have been discharged perfectly recovered,* and

21, so much improved, as not to require further confinement.

The remaining thirty recent cases, have been of the melancholic class ; of whom,

5 have died,

4 remain in the house,

19 have been discharged perfectly recovered, and

2, so much improved, as not to require further confinement.

The old, or what are usually termed, incurable cases, which have been admitted, consist of sixty-one of the maniacal, twenty-one of the melancholic class, and six cases of dementia. Of the former,

---

* Patients who have recovered, and have returned to the Institution *relapsed*, are not noticed in this summary as being recovered; unless they have finally been discharged in that state. No case of this kind, is considered as forming more than one instance of admission or recovery.

11 have died,

31 remain in the house *,

  5 have been removed by their friends improved,

10 have been discharged perfectly recovered, and

  4, so much improved, as not to require further confinement.

Of the twenty-one melancholics,

  6 have died,

  6 remain in the house,

  1 has been removed by the friends of the patient, somewhat improved,

  6 have been discharged perfectly recovered, and

  2, so much improved, as not to require further confinement.

Of the six cases of dementia,

  2 have died,

  2 have been discharged as not suitable objects, and

  2 remain in the house.

The present master of St. Luke's Hospital, stated, in the year 1807, before a select committee of the House of Commons, on " the state of Lunatics," that " the average number of curable patients ad-

---

* Several of these are improved, as may be seen in the table.

mitted annually is as follows : Males 110. Females 153. Total 263. The numbers discharged are as follows : Cured, Males 37. Females 71. Total 108. Uncured, Males and Females 100. Unfit from various causes, 28. Dead 27."

Haslam, the apothecary to Bethlem Hospital, states, that in a period of ten years, from 1784 to 1794, 1664 patients were admitted ; of whom 574 were discharged cured, and 1090, uncured. It appears also, from the same authority, that " In the course of the last twenty years, seventy-eight patients," who had been ill more than twelve months, " have been received, of whom only one has been discharged cured. This patient, who was a woman, has since relapsed twice, and was ultimately sent from the hospital uncured *."

The same author informs us, that " patients who are in a furious state, recover in a larger proportion than those who are melancholic. An hundred violent, and the same number of melancholic cases, were selected : of the former, sixty-two were discharged

----

* Observations on Madness, p. 251.

well; of the latter, only twenty-seven: subsequent experience has confirmed this fact." *

We learn from an interesting paper, by Dr. Pinel, in the Journal de Physique †, that in the hospital de la Salpêtriere in France, 1002 patients were admitted, in three years and nine months; of whom 473 were discharged cured. It is proper to state, that of the 1002 patients, 388 had been previously under care in other hospitals; and it does not appear certain that the rest were all of them recent cases.

It is obvious, that we cannot form a just estimate of the importance of the curative means, employed in different asylums, from a bare comparison of the numbers stated to be admitted, and to be discharged, as cured, from each.

Before we attempt to draw any inference from reports of this kind, it is necessary to inquire particularly,

---

* Page 257.

† Tome lxvii. Septembre, an 1808.

I. The principal causes of the disease in the cases admitted into the establishments, whose statements we are comparing.

II. The rules of the establishment, in regard to the admission of old or recent cases, and also in respect of the dismissal of patients.

III. The precise meaning of the terms employed in the Reports, especially that of cured or recovered.

I will venture to offer a few remarks on each of these heads, to enable the reader to judge of the peculiar circumstances of our establishment; and that he may compare with greater advantage the report here exhibited, with the statements of other hospitals.

I. OF THE CAUSES OF THE DISEASE.

It is extremely difficult to obtain correct infor mation upon this subject. The delicacy or negligence of the friends of the patients, forms a considerable impediment; but where these do not arise, and when what is conceived to be the exciting cause, is freely stated, there is frequently great reason to suspect, that the imputed cause is, in reality, no more than the first overt act, sufficiently characteristic to force attention.

The approach of a maniacal paroxysm, is generally marked by an uncommon flow of spirits, and great warmth of the passions. For a time, these are not unusually kept in considerable subjection; but the mind, in this state, seeks for situations unfavourable to its calmness. The mental excitement of some, leads them to form indiscreet and hasty attachments, which, leading to disappointment, hastens or perhaps induces the complete developement of the disorder. Some rush into imprudent commercial engagements; and others devote themselves to religious speculations. These often run from one place of worship to another, preferring those where the passions are most excited. Hence arises the ambiguity, which obtains in regard to most of the moral causes of insanity.

It will be seen by a reference to the list of Apparent Causes, in the preceding table, that a large number of the cases admitted into our establishment, have been connected with some strong mental emotion, to which the disorder has been attributed. The human mind does not like uncertainty; and the relatives of the insane, are generally anxious to fix on some particular circumstance, as the cause of disease. To imagine it to be a constitutional malady, gives to it a character of hopelessness, from which our pride and our affection alike recoil. In several instances, however, where the cause has been decidedly expressed, a more accurate history of the paroxysm and previous habits of the patient, has led to conclusions, widely different from those which had been formed by more partial, or less inquisitive friends.

The instances attributed to disappointed affections, which have occurred in the Retreat, form, perhaps, about the same proportion to the whole, that they do in other similar establishments; and nearly all writers agree, in declaring the great ambiguity of this apparent cause of insanity.

Very few of the cases admitted into the Retreat, have been, in their commencement, at all connected with religious impressions; and in most of the cases which have occurred, inquiry has proved, that the unhappy religious notions, have not been excited by any external means; but have arisen spontaneously in the mind ; and have been either preceded or attended by other symptoms of approaching insanity.

In one instance, the disorder came on during the singing in a Methodist meeting-house ; but an extraordinary excitement had been previously ob-served ; which, it is at least highly probable, led the patient to the place where the ebullition of his mind, could no longer be repressed.

This is one of the cases which, in vulgar estima-tion, is attributable to the Methodists ; and if the *apothecary* of Bethlem Hospital, who professes himself under great obligations to this sect, for a great proportion of his patients, had an opportunity of fully investigating the origin of similar cases, he would probably find himself not so much indebted to Methodism, as he at present imagines ; and his remarks upon this head, would perhaps be found equally just with his observation, that " the decorous piety, and exemplary life of the Quaker, has signally exempted him from this most severe of human infirmities." The *surgeon* to Bethlem Hospital says : " As for the opinion which some entertain, of the prevalent effect of Methodism, in producing insanity, proof, in place of bold and bare assertion, is required to settle this point." * We may, however, conclude, from the statements of the apothecary, that religious impressions have been the *apparent* cause of disorder in a great number of the patients admitted into Bethlem Hospital; which certainly has not been the case at the Retreat. In this respect, therefore, a material difference obtains, with regard to the prevalent causes of disease, in the two Institutions; and, consequently, before a just comparison can be made, it will be necessary to decide the probability of cure, in cases of insanity, apparently arising from religious impressions. Haslam considers the disease, under these circumstances, as peculiarly incorrigible; and the cases which have been admitted under notice at the Retreat, are too few to enable us to form a general opinion. Only three cases have occurred, which can at all be considered as coming under this description; but it is worthy of remark, that two of them have been completely recovered, and the other considerably improved.

Intemperance is another very prevalent, and less ambiguous cause of insanity, in most public In-

---

* Crowther's Practical Remarks, p. 85.

stitutions. This has not, however, been the occasion of disorder in more than three of the cases admitted into the Retreat. In one of these, the habit had become inveterate; but the violence and intensity of the mind upon all subjects which interested it, had long previously marked a constitutional tendency to the disease. This patient was discharged improved, but he still requires care. The other two patients both recovered. Haslam, however, considers intemperance as one of the more unfavourable causes of the disorder.

In several cases admitted into the Retreat, the disorder has been obviously connected with epilepsy; and it is so well known, that such cases rarely admit of relief, that they are not admitted into St. Luke's hospital. I am not aware that the prevalent causes of disease, in the cases admitted into our establishment, differ from the generality of similar places in other respects, than those which I have already stated.

It will, I trust, be readily admitted, that the habits and principles of the Society of Friends, are at least not more unfriendly to mental sanity, than those of other societies; and this opinion will derive some confirmation, from observing the large number of cases, in which the disease has been ascertained to be constitutional or hereditary. In a great number of instances, information on this head could not be obtained ; and we may therefore safely presume, that the proportion is considerably larger than appears in the statements.

II. OF THE RULES OF THE ESTABLISHMENT, &c.

The object of the Retreat, being to furnish a comfortable shelter for insane persons, as well as to promote their recovery, its original rules made no distinction between old and recent cases; and did not, in any degree, limit the time of patients' continuance in the house. The only restriction relates to idiots ; and this appears to have been generally understood as applying, chiefly, to cases of original absence of intellect.

In these respects, the circumstances of this establishment, differ materially from those of some of our largest public institutions.

It appears, from the statement of the master of St. Luke's Hospital, made before a Committee of the

House of Commons, that, in this Institution, " The average number of patients at one time is 300 ;" and that " the average number of incurable patients, in the house at one time, is 115." All patients are discharged from this Asylum at the end of the first year; and if not then recovered, may be entered on the incurable list, to be admitted when a vacancy offers; but it appears that only a certain number of this class of patients are permitted to be in the house at one time. The rules of this hospital do not admit patients, " troubled with epileptic or convulsive fits."

By the following quotation from Haslam, it appears, that the rules of Bethlem Hospital guard against the admission of old cases: "Although patients who have been affected with insanity more than a year, are not admissible into the hospital, to continue there for the usual time of trial for cure, viz. a twelvemonth ; yet, at the discretion of the Committee, they may be received into it from Lady-day to Michaelmas ; at which latter period they are removed. In the course of the last twenty years, seventy-eight patients of this description have been received."

There are, however, a number of patients in Bethlem, who have been there many years ; and I

P

therefore conclude, that a certain proportion is permitted, as in St. Luke's, to remain on the incurable establishment.—But, as Haslam states, that from the year 1784 to 1794, out of 1664 cases admitted, 1090 were discharged uncured, I presume that the number of patients in this hospital, who have been afflicted with insanity more than a year, is comparatively very small.

It will be seen that a large majority of the cases admitted into the Retreat, have not been recent. In several instances, the disorder had existed from fifteen to twenty years previously to their admission ; and, of course, no reasonable hope could be entertained of the patients' recovery. The total proportion of cures cannot, therefore, be expected to be large. I will not, however, omit to mention, that the number of these must have been fewer, if the rules had limited the time of continuance in the house, as is the case in the two charitable Institutions above mentioned. But, it must also be observed, that several patients who have been sane at the expiration of twelve months, have remained in the house from three to six months longer on probation, or *at their own request*, until a suitable situation offered for them.

Others, who have been apparently well at the end of twelve months, have relapsed before they quitted the house; and I cannot avoid attributing to the premature discharge of insane persons, many of the relapses which occur after they leave the places provided for their care. Several of the symptoms which mark the disorder in its incipient state, also mark an advanced stage of convalescence. In either case, though no absolute act of insanity is committed, the mind is unable to bear that stimulus or exertion, which would be even salutary to it, in a state of perfect sanity.

III. EXPLANATION OF TERMS.

It will have been observed that the cases, in the preceding tables, are arranged under three classes, viz. Dementia, Melancholia, and Mania.

The first comprehends those cases in which the mental powers appear materially weakened; which are attended with a general irritability, or are subject to occasional maniacal paroxysms, rendering the patients dangerous to themselves or others. Idiocy, or mere imbecility of mind, as has been already stated, is not admissible into the Retreat; though persons who sink into that state, are not necessarily discharged.

P 2

Under the class, Melancholia, all cases are included, in which the disorder is chiefly marked by depression of mind, whether it is, or is not, attended by general false notions. Those cases, however, are distinguished, in which the melancholy feelings are immediately connected with hypochondriasis.

In the third class, Mania, all those cases are included, in which the disorder is not chiefly marked by weakness of intellect, or mental depression.

In regard to the division of the cases into old and recent, it will be proper to observe, that those of more than twelve months standing, are considered under the former, and all the others under the latter division.

I know not what degree of sanity is generally thought sufficient to warrant the application of the term, ' cured.' In the preceding tables, the term *recovered*, is applied only where the patient is fully competent to fulfil his common duties, or is restored to the state he was in, previously to the attack.

As we have not discovered any antimaniacal specific, and profess to do little more than assist Nature, in the performance of her own cure, the term *recovered*, is adopted in preference to that of *cured*.

I will conclude this chapter by considering, whether insanity is essentially prejudicial to animal life.

Dr. Monro, in his reply to Dr. Battie's Treatise on Madness, gives the following evidence upon this subject : " Although I do not remember to have seen more than four instances, where I could say, the fury of madness was the immediate occasion of death, I have great reason to believe that madness destroys two-thirds of those, who are afflicted with it through life. *"

Dr. Crichton † tells us that, " melancholic patients seldom live long. They often terminate their own existence in the attacks of the disorder; but, even when carefully watched, and when every care is taken of them, they *never* attain old age. Many die before thirty or forty ; and few live beyond sixty ; but a great deal of diversity, in this respect, arises from the difference of the time of life when they are first

---

* Page 26.

† An Inquiry into the Nature and Origin of Mental Derangement, by Alexander Crichton, M. D. Vol. II. p. 236.

seized with the complaint."—Dr. C. refers us in this place to " Greding's Aphorisms," which form an Appendix to his work.   It is there stated, that " the greater number of insane people fall into a state of atrophy, or decay, towards the close of their life: for it has been found, that of one hundred maniacs, sixty-eight died in this way; of twenty-six epileptic maniacs, there were thirteen; of sixteen epileptic idiots, only four; and of twenty-four melancholic, there were twenty; and lastly, of thirty idiots, there were twenty-one who died of this kind of con-sumption."

The next sentence states " Hydrothorax to be the disease to which they are *most* subject;" and a suc-ceeding aphorism informs us, that " consumption, from an ulcerated state of the lungs, appears to be another disease which *often* terminates the existence of insane people."   Not to dwell on the seeming contradiction in these statements; that two distinct diseases are each of them represented as being the *most* frequent occasion of death among insane per-sons, it is perhaps matter of doubt, whether the frequency of these diseases, is not more connected with the mode of treatment, than with the mental disorder.

Of the twenty-six deaths which have occurred in the Retreat since its establishment, a period of 16 years, three have been in consequence of epilepsy, and two of apoplexy, with which the patients were affected previously to their admission, and which appeared to be the causes of derangement. Seven patients have died in a state of atrophy; but of these, three appeared to be in the last stage of decay at the time of their admission. Three patients have died of general dropsy, two of inflammation of the intestines, two of external inflammation, one of hemorrhage from the stomach, one of erysipelas, one of convulsions, and one of fever. Three cases, in which the unhappy disposition of the patient to injure himself, proved fatal, complete the statement of causes of mortality in this Institution. It is no small satisfaction to be able to add, that the three melancholy cases just mentioned, are the only instances of the kind; and that in the last eight years, during which the average number of patients has been fifty-six, no circumstance of this kind has occurred.

It may be proper to state, that the average number of patients in this Institution at one time, since its establishment, is 46; and the following summary shows the ages of the patients at present in the house:

15 to 20 years inclusive 2

20 to 30 8

30 to 40 12

40 to 50 20

50 to 60 7

60 to 70 11

70 to 80 4

80 to 90 2

One of the patients is 87 years of age; and it is remarkable, has been subject to very frequent and violent paroxysms of vociferous mania, during the last ten years.

The number of deaths, in this Institution, is too small to admit any decided inferences to be drawn, as to the general causes of mortality amongst insane persons; but the ages of those now in the house, as well as the general result in regard to the number of deaths, will perhaps fully justify an opinion, that insanity is not essentially prejudicial to animal life.

APPENDIX.

◆

THE Author hopes he shall be justified in presenting the reader with the sentiments of some respectable persons, who have carefully inspected the Retreat. His view in doing so, is to confirm the testimony which he has given in the preceding pages, of the practices of this Institution, and which might be suspected of partiality, if it were not supported by the evidence of disinterested persons, who were qualified to judge on the occasion.

In the year 1798, Dr. DELARIVE, of Geneva, after having examined a great number of public and private establishments of a similar nature, visited the Retreat. It was then in its infancy, but, the Doctor was so far pleased with the general management, as to write a very favourable description of it, in a letter addressed to the editors of " The British Library." This letter afterwards appeared on the Continent in a separate form*, from a copy of which the following extracts are made.

After describing the evils which have existed in the treatment of the insane in public hospitals, which he observes would lead one to suppose, that madmen were employed in tormenting other madmen, he says, " The respectable society of Quakers have at length endeavoured to remedy these evils; it has been desirous of securing to

---

* Lettre adressée aux Rédacteurs de la Bibliothèque Britannique sur un nouvel etablissement pour la guerison des Aliénés.

those of its members, who should have the unhappiness to lose their reason, without possessing a fortune adequate to have recourse to expensive establishments, all the resources of art, and all the comforts of life, compatible with their situation. A voluntary subscription furnished the funds; and, about two years since, an establishment, which appears to unite many advantages, with all possible economy, was founded near the city of York.

" If the mind shrinks for a moment at the aspect of this terrible disease, which seems calculated to humble the reason of man; it must afterwards feel pleasing emotions, in considering all that an ingenious benevolence has been able to invent, to cure and comfort the patients afflicted with this malady.

" This house is situated a mile from York, in the midst of a fertile and cheerful country; it presents not the idea of a prison, but rather that of a large rural farm. It is surrounded by a garden. There is no bar or grating to the windows, their place is supplied by a means of which I shall afterwards give an account." *

---

* " La respectable Société des Quakers a essayé dernièrement de remédier à ces maux; elle a desiré assurer à ceux de ses Membres qui auroient le malheur de perdre la raison sans avoir une fortune suffisante pour recourir aux établissemens dispendieux, toutes les ressources de l'art et toutes les douceurs de la vie compatibles avec leur état; une souscription volontaire a fourni les fonds, et depuis deux ans environ, un établissement qui paroit réunir beaucoup d'avantages avec toute l'économie possible, a été fondé près de la ville d'York. Si l'ame se flétrit un moment à l'aspect de cette terrible maladie qui semble faite pour humilier la raison humaine, on éprouve ensuite de douces émotions en considérant tout ce qu'une bienveillance ingénieuse a sû inventer pour la guérir ou la soulager.

" Cette

After a general view of the economy of the Retreat, and the general treatment of the patients, the Doctor thus concludes his letter:—" You will perceive that in the moral treatment of the insane, they do not consider them as absolutely deprived of reason; or, in other words, as inaccessible to the motives of fear, hope, feeling, and honour. It appears, that they consider them rather as children, who have too much strength, and who make a dangerous use of it. Their punishments and rewards must be immediate, since that which is distant has no effect upon them. A new system of education must be adopted to give a fresh course to their ideas. Subject them at first;* encourage them afterwards, employ them, and render their employment agreeable by attractive means. I think that if we could find still stronger means to excite feelings of benevolence in their minds, we should accelerate their recovery by the agreeable emotions which accompany all the affections. But it is evident, that every needless restraint, excites in them the vindictive passions, to which they are but too prone, and prolongs the continuance of the disease." †

" Cette maison est située à un mille de York au mileau d'une campagne fertile et riante: ce n'est point l'idée d'une prison qu'elle fait naître, mais plutôt celle d'une grande ferme rustique, elle est entourée d'un jardin fermé. Point de barreau, point de grillages aux fenètres, on y a suppléé par un moyen dont je rendrai compte ci-après."—P. 5, 6.

* If this maxim was ever acted upon at the Retreat, it is now in great measure exploded. See page 146.

† " Vous voyez, que dans le traitement moral on ne considere pas les fous comme absolument prives de raison, c'est-à-dire, comme inaccessibles aux motifs

de

A FEW years since, W. STARK, Esq. Architect, of Glasgow, who was engaged to prepare a plan of an Asylum for that city and the west of Scotland, visited the Retreat. The following extract is made from his valuable " Remarks on the Construction and Management of Lunatic Asylums," published in the year 1810. " In some asylums, which I have visited, chains are affixed to every table, and to every bed-post; in others, they are not to be found within the walls. The idea of inflicting corporal punishment is held in abhorrence; and rods or whips are considered as engines of power, too dreadful to be committed to the hands of servants, who may soon convert them into instruments of oppression.

" In such asylums, however, there are no appearances of insubordination. The whole demeanour of the patients, on the contrary, is most remarkably submissive and orderly. The one to which I especially allude, the Retreat, or Quaker Asylum, near York, it may be proper to mention, is occupied by a description

---

de crainte, d'espérance, de sentimens et d'honneur. On les considere plutôt, ce semble, comme des enfans qui ont un superflu de force et qui en faisoient un emploi dangereux. Il leur faut des peines et des récompenses présentes : tout ce qui est un peu éloigné n'a point d'effet sur eux. Il faut leur appliquer un nouveau système d'éducation, donner un nouveau cours à leurs idées ; les subjuguer d'abord, les encourager ensuite, les appliquer au travail, leur rendre ce travail agréable par des moyens attrayans. Je pense que si on pouvoit encore trouver des mobiles plus forts pour exciter en eux la bienveillance, on accéléreroit leur rétablissement par les sentimens agréables qui accompagnent toutes les affections sociales. Mais on sent bien au moins que toute contrainte inutile, excitant chez eux les passions vindicatives auxquelles ils ne sont que trop portés, prolonge la durée de la maladie."—P. 29, 30.

of people, whose usual habits in life are highly regular and exemplary; but the chief cause of its superiority will be found to lie in the government of the asylum. It is a goverment of humanity and of consummate skill, and requires no aid from the arm of violence, or the exertions of brutal force.

" At the Retreat, they sometimes have patients brought to them, frantic, and in irons, whom they at once release, and, by mild arguments and gentle arts, reduce almost immediately to obedience and orderly behaviour. A great deal of delicacy appears in the attentions paid to the smaller feelings of the patients. The iron bars, which guarded the windows, have been avoided, and neat iron sashes, having all the appearance of wooden ones, have been substituted in their place; and, when I visited them, the managers were occupied in contriving how to get rid of the bolts with which the patients are shut up at night, on account of their harsh ungrateful sound, and of their communicating to the asylum somewhat of the air and character of a prison.

" The effects of such attentions, both on the happiness of the patients, and the discipline of the Institution, are more important than may at first view be imagined. Attachment to the place and to the managers, and an air of comfort and of contentment, rarely exhibited within the precincts of such establishments, are consequences easily discovered in the general demeanour of the patients." *

The following testimony is extracted from an account lately published of the Lunatic Asylum at Edinburgh? and we are

* Pages 11, 12.

authorized to state, that it comes from the pen of Dr. DUNCAN, sen. who visited the Retreat in the year 1812, after having seen most of the Institutions of a similar nature in Britain.

" That the government of the Insane requires a certain degree of restraint, both for the safety of the individual and of others, no one can doubt. But very different opinions have been entertained with regard to the utmost degree of coercion, which is necessary in any case. Now, however, this point may be considered as in some degree settled by experience. The fraternity denominated Quakers have demonstrated, beyond contradiction, the very great advantage resulting from a mode of treatment in cases of Insanity, much more mild than was before introduced into almost any Lunatic Asylum, either at home or abroad. That fraternity, who have been long and justly celebrated for charity and humanity, have established in the neighbourhood of the City of York, *The Retreat*, as they term it, a building appropriated to deranged members of their own community. In the management of this Institution, they have set an example which claims the imitation, and deserves the thanks, of every sect and every nation. For, without much hazard of contradiction from those acquainted with the subject, it may be asserted, that the Retreat at York, is at this moment the best-regulated establishment in Europe, either for the recovery of the insane, or for their comfort, where they are in an incurable state."*

DR. NAUDI, president of the Maltese Hospitals, after carefully inspecting the Retreat in the present year, gave the following testimony respecting it:

* Page 15.

" I am very glad to have been at York, to observe the Retreat there, kept by the Society of Friends. This house, or Retreat, for the troubled in mind, I think is one of the best things I saw in England on the same subject; and having observed many others on the Continent, I dare say that it is the best in all the world. The situation of the building out of the town, a large garden around it, the propriety of the rooms, the cleanliness of the patients, the way in which they are kept, as for dressing, as for feeding them, is very remarkable to be observed." *

---

* Dr. N. had studied the English language, only nine months.

THE END.

From the Office of
THOMAS WILSON and SONS,
High-Ousegate, York.

Errata.

On the Ground Plan in all the courts, for *yards*, read *square yards*.

Page 108, line 2, for *induces* read *induce*.

———

DIRECTIONS FOR THE BINDER.

Perspective Elevation .... to face the Title page.

Ground Plan .... to face ...... page 95.

Second Floor .... to face ...... page 100.

To be fixed with a guard, in the middle.